Documents and Debates
The Normans in Britain

Documents and Debates
General Editor: John Wroughton M.A., F.R.Hist.S.

The Normans in Britain

Donald Wilkinson

John Cantrell
The Manchester Grammar School

MACMILLAN
EDUCATION

First published 1987

Published by
MACMILLAN EDUCATION LTD
Houndmills, Basingstoke, Hampshire RG21 2XS
and London
Companies and representatives
throughout the world

Typeset by Wessex Typesetters
(Division of The Eastern Press Ltd)
Frome, Somerset

Printed in Hong Kong

British Library Cataloguing in Publication Data
The Normans in Britain.—(Documents and debates)
1. Great Britain—History—Norman period, 1066–1154
I. Wilkinson, Donald   II. Cantrell, John
III. Series
942.02   DA195
ISBN 0–333–39871–8

Contents

General Editor's Preface

This book forms part of a series entitled *Documents and Debates*, which is aimed primarily at sixth formers. The earlier volumes in the series each covered approximately one century of history, using material both from original documents and from modern historians. The more recent volumes, however, are designed in response to the changing trends in history examinations at 18 plus, most of which now demand the study of documentary sources and the testing of historical skills. Each volume therefore concentrates on a particular topic within a narrower span of time. It consists of eight sections, each dealing with a major theme in depth, illustrated by extracts drawn from primary sources. The series intends partly to provide experience for those pupils who are required to answer questions on documentary material at A-level, and partly to provide pupils of all abilities with a digestible and interesting collection of source material, which will extend the normal textbook approach.

This book is designed essentially for the pupil's own personal use. The author's introduction will put the period as a whole into perspective, highlighting the central issues, main controversies, available source material and recent developments. Although it is clearly not our intention to replace the traditional textbook, each section will carry its own brief introduction, which will set the documents into context. A wide variety of source material has been used in order to give the pupils the maximum amount of experience – letters, speeches, newspapers, memoirs, diaries, official papers, Acts of Parliament, Minute Books, accounts, local documents, family papers, etc. The questions vary in difficulty, but aim throughout to compel the pupil to think in depth by the use of unfamiliar material. Historical knowledge and understanding will be tested, as well as basic comprehension. Pupils will also be encouraged by the questions to assess the reliability of evidence, to recognise bias and emotional prejudice, to reconcile conflicting accounts and to extract the essential from the irrelevant. Some questions, *marked with an asterisk*, require knowledge outside the immediate extract and are intended for further research or discussion, based on the pupil's general knowledge of the period. Finally, we hope that students using this material will learn something of the nature of historical inquiry and the role of the historian.

John Wroughton

Acknowledgements

The author and publishers wish to thank the following who have kindly given permission for the use of copyright material;

Edward Arnold Ltd for extracts from *The Norman Conquest* (Documents of Medieval History series) by Allen R. Brown (1984)

Associated Book Publishers (UK) Ltd for extracts from *English Historical Documents II 1042–1189* eds D. C. Douglas and G. W. Greenaway, Eyre and Spottiswoode; and *William Rufus* by Frank Barlow, Methuen, London (1983)

Les Belles Lettres for extracts from *Vie de Louis VI Le Gros* by Suger, ed. and trans. Henri Waquet (1964)

Cambridge University Press for an extract from *The Church and the Two Nations in Medieval Ireland* by J. A. Watt (1970)

Century Hutchinson Ltd for extracts from *Eadmer's History of Recent Events in England* trans. Geoffrey Bosanquet, Cresset Press (1964)

J. M. Dent & Sons Ltd for extracts from *The Anglo-Saxon Chronicles* trans. G. N. Garmonsway, Everyman's Library (1953)

Institute of Historical Research and J. A. Green for table from 'The Earliest Surviving Pipe Roll', *Bulletin of the Institute of Historical Research*, vol. LV (1982)

The Medieval Academy of America for Appendix A, Part 1 from 'Patronage in the Pipe Roll of 1130' by Stephanie Mooers, *Speculum: A Journal of Medieval Studies*, vol. 59 (1984)

Oxford University Press for extracts from The Ecclesiastical History of Orderic Vitalis, ed. and trans. Marjorie Chibnall (1969), *The Carmen de Hastingae Proelio of Guy, Bishop of Amiens*, eds. and trans. Catherine Morton and Hope Muntz (1972), *Letters of Lanfranc, Archbishop of Canterbury*, eds and trans. Helen Glover and Margaret Gibson (1979), *Gesta Stephani* ed. and trans. K. R. Potter (1976), *De Nugis Curialium* by Walter Mapp, ed. and trans. M. R. James, revised by C. N. L. Brooke and R. A. B. Mynors (1983); and from *Vita Ædwardi Regis*, ed. and trans. F. Barlow (1962), *Hugh the Chantor: The History of the Church of York 1066–1127* trans. C. Johnson (1961), *William of Malmesbury: Historia Novella* trans. K. R. Potter (1955), Oxford Medieval Texts series (formerly the Nelson Medieval Texts)

The Normans in Britain, 1066–1154

Introduction

1066, according to W. C. Sellar and R. J. Yeatman, provided 'the other memorable date in English History . . . the Norman Conquest was a Good Thing, as from this time onwards England stopped being conquered and thus was able to become top nation'.[1] The now rather dated humour of *1066 And All That* still encapsulates one aspect of the major controversy which has flourished around the Conquest almost since it occurred – that the Conquest decisively changed the pattern of historical development in England. R. Allen Brown, in more academic tenor, has declared that 'the Norman Conquest was a turning-point in the history of England, and only less dramatically in the history of Western Europe and of Latin Christendom'. He does not deny that elements of continuity between Anglo-Saxon and Norman England exist, but believes that these should not be overemphasised, for 'the Norman Conquest involved, whatever else, a revolution in the upper levels of society, a complete change of personnel at the top, the imposition of a new and alien ruling dynasty and ruling class'. Brown pushes the discontinuity argument still further when he concludes his examination of the effects of the Conquest by quoting Carlyle's often-cited question: 'England itself, in foolish quarters of England, still howls and execrates lamentably over its William Conqueror, and rigorous line of Normans and Plantagenets; but without them, if you will consider well, what had it ever been'.[2] This cataclysmic view of the Conquest has not gone unchallenged, and many now echo, if not with the same strength of patriotic feeling or racial undertones, the words of the Victorian historian, E. A. Freeman, who still described the Conquest as 'a turning-point', but attached a different meaning to his interpretation of that word. 'The Norman Conquest', he wrote, 'brought with it a most extensive foreign infusion, an infusion which affected our blood, our language, our laws, our arts; still it was only an infusion; the older and stronger elements still survived, and in the long run they again made good their supremacy.'[3] F. M. Stenton, who did more than any other historian to rediscover the vitality of Anglo-Saxon England, remarked that the Normans, at first, did much 'to disguise the fact of conquest', and that 'the framework of the Old English state survived the Conquest', although he was finally forced to admit that in spite of the evidence of continuity, 'the fact remains that sooner or later every aspect of English life was changed by the Norman Conquest'.[4]

However, the controversy is not quite so simple and to view the events of the later eleventh century in the light of the Conquest alone is to mislead. For the later eleventh century was a time of rapid development throughout Europe which saw many countries transformed. And, as a recent general survey of medieval British history has remarked, 'there is the problem. In some respects 1066 wrought great changes; in other respects, great changes occurred but can hardly be ascribed to the Conquest; in yet others, the most striking feature is not change at all, but continuity.'[5]

The question of how far the Normans brought change or were absorbed into the continuum of development from Anglo-Saxon England can only be considered by examining the evidence which survives from the period. From the late eleventh century there was a tremendous proliferation of written records. Although the Anglo-Saxon Chronicle came to be continued at only one monastery after 1070, it was joined by a burgeoning of historical writing amongst other monks. The major chronicles are well represented in this volume in that they provide the majority of the extracts. But many narrative sources do not lend themselves easily to brief quotation and there is no substitute for reading the chronicles extensively. Only then can the full flavour of the writings of men like William of Malmesbury and Orderic Vitalis be appreciated. It is also important to know something about the background of these writers in order to assess the value of their evidence, and so a brief note on the major chronicles cited in this volume is included at the end of the book.

Writs and charters exist in greater abundance from the time of the Conquest than from any time previously. These 'record' sources together with official acts of government are more difficult to use in a work of this type because much of the true value to be gained from them can only be obtained by studying them in large numbers: attestations to royal writs or charters, for instance, can provide important evidence about the composition of the royal court and the distribution of patronage, but it is probably most useful in examining the court over a period of time, something which is beyond the scope of this volume. However, the memorable official records of government are not ignored and examples of what can be found in the Domesday Book and the Pipe Roll of 1130 are to be found in the chapters on the effects of the Conquest and on the rule of Henry I. Other types of evidence are also included to give a glimpse of the material that is available. For example, the Bayeux Tapestry is invaluable for what it can tell us about the Conquest, while Lanfranc was a letter writer of distinction, whose correspondence allows us a view of the scholarly, but practical man he must have been.

As the Editor's Preface remarks, this series of books is not a substitute for textbooks, monographs or articles. This volume is an introduction only to some of the concerns of the period, and we have tried to pick out different types of controversy and problem in each chapter so that the reader, coming to the period early in his historical career, has the chance to sample some of the diversity of the Anglo-Norman era.

Frequent succession disputes were an inevitable consequence of a time when laws of inheritance were unclear and the contingencies of demographic survival very uncertain. This was most obviously the case in 1066 as Chapter 1 reveals, but the centrality of inheritance and laws of succession runs through the whole of the Anglo-Norman period and recurs in several chapters, notably Chapter 5 on the death of William Rufus. The process of Conquest and the effects of military victory on the economy and society are major concerns of historians examining the reign of the Conqueror, and so Chapters 2 and 4 are devoted largely to these questions. The vexed debate over feudalism obviously looms large here. The security of the regime was not something William I alone was concerned about. Henry I and Stephen had to try to consolidate their rules, particularly in view of the circumstances in which they attained the throne. Chapters 6 and 7 look at some aspects of the complexities of the reigns of Henry I and Stephen, notably the way in which each ruler tried to maintain his power. Of course, no study of the Anglo-Norman period would be complete without some reference to the great religious controversies of the time. Chapter 3 looks at some of the evidence for the Norman reforms of the Church, the disputes at the Council of Rockingham and the great Investiture Controversy. Norman interest in Britain was not confined to England alone, and Chapter 8 illustrates Norman involvement with the Welsh, the Scots, and, to a much lesser extent, the Irish. This chapter also introduces a reminder that the Normans were, probably primarily, concerned with Normandy. The Anglo-Norman state was a cross-Channel state and, without proper acceptance of this central fact, understanding of the Normans' activities in Britain will be impossible.

Through nearly all these chapters two themes predominate. One is the importance of war to the Normans. For they were, as William of Malmesbury remarked, 'a race inured to war, and can hardly live without it'.[6] Battle and military might often dictated the path of their development. The development of Norman institutions of government was heavily influenced by the need to allow the royal military machine to function effectively. The other theme is the role of personality and the significance of personal relationships in Anglo-Norman affairs. We will never know what the Normans were like as people as modern biographers can know their subjects, but the importance of trying to gain some understanding of their characters is vital to any assessment of them or their activities. Personal relationships lay at the core of the patronage system. The successful operation of this determined the success or failure of all medieval kings. The patronage system looms larger in the writing of medieval history as written records increase, but its importance in the Anglo-Norman state cannot be denied as the Pipe Roll of 1130 tantalisingly shows.

Finally, a word should be said about the nature of the questions and their relationship to the extracts. Documentary work of the type contained in this book has become fashionable at all levels of schooling, and in school examinations especially. Examinations tend to breed the assumption that 'right answers' exist, however erroneous that assumption might in fact be. Documentary work of this type has also been promoted by the direct and indirect influence of the Schools Council History Project. One of its successful productions was to push the idea of the historian as detective. However, this analogy cannot and should not be pushed too far. Overemphasis on limited numbers of documents and questions set on them can also lead the unwary to suspect that history is a subject of 'right answers' and legalistic-type proofs. This is, of course, untrue. History is about interpretation of the evidence which has survived from a particular period. The survival of evidence is also partial, and is especially so in the Anglo-Norman era. The questions are designed to provoke discussion and a desire to investigate further the problems put forward here. For the historian can only aim 'at explanations which approximate to unverifiable truth' or, put differently, 'constructs of persuasive possibility'.[7] It is an awareness of this difficulty in the light of the Anglo-Norman period that this book desires most to promote, and it is something that should be borne in mind in making an assessment of the Anglo-Norman period as a whole. The Norman contribution to Britain was affected not only by the innovations the Normans themselves brought, but also by the continuities which remained from the Anglo-Saxon kingdom, by other extraneous developments, and by the changes which would be wrought in the future by the Angevins and their successors. For, as F. Barlow remarked in an essay published to mark the nine hundredth anniversary of the Battle of Hastings, 'it is probable that much of the Norman contribution to the English way of life only became significant because there was an Angevin "conquest" in 1154 . . . . In 1153 the new kingdom was inchoate, diversified, inconsistent, capable of several different developments . . .'.[8] It is hoped that the extracts in this book will begin to introduce the reader to something of this diversity and complexity.

Notes

1 W. C. Sellar and R. J. Yeatman, *1066 And All That* (35th edn, London, 1951), pp 16–17. The other date was 55 B.C.
2 R. Allen Brown, *The Normans and the Norman Conquest* (London, Boydell, 1969), pp 203, 204, 264.
3 E. A. Freeman, *The History of the Norman Conquest* (3rd edn, 6 vols, Oxford, 1877), vol. i, p 1.
4 F. M. Stenton, *Anglo-Saxon England* (3rd edn, Oxford, O.U.P., 1971), pp 622, 683, 686.
5 J. Gillingham, 'The Early Middle Ages (1066–1290)', in *The Sphere Illustrated History of Britain, c. 55 B.C.–1485*, ed. K. O. Morgan (London, Sphere Books, 1985), p 118.
6 Quoted in R. Allen Brown, op cit, p 264.
7 G. R. Elton quoted in M. R. Horowitz, 'Which road to the past?', *History Today*, vol. 34 (Jan. 1984), p 10.
8 F. Barlow, 'The Effects of the Norman Conquest', in F. Barlow, *The Norman Conquest and Beyond* (London, Hambledon Press, 1983), pp 186–7.

I   Prelude to Conquest

Introduction

The death of King Edward the Confessor on 5 January 1066 unleashed one of the most bitter and hotly contested succession disputes in English history. The prize was a rich and prosperous island strategically placed between the competing rulers of Scandinavia and Europe; 50 years of peace had led to expanding trade and industry and certain centres of population had grown large enough to be called towns. The claimants to this attractive inheritance included two Scandinavian kings, Harald Hardraada and Svein Estrithson of Norway and Denmark respectively, an English royal prince, Edgar Aetheling, and the two principal protagonists Harold Godwinson, Earl of Wessex, and William, Duke of Normandy. Although the issue was finally resolved on the battlefields of Yorkshire and Sussex during the autumn of 1066, the English succession had been a growing problem for at least the previous fifteen years. In fact, if Edward the Confessor had determined to maintain a celibate marriage, it was a problem from the beginning of his reign.

There were good reasons why the Confessor should have favoured his second cousin, Duke William: Edward's mother, Emma, was the daughter of Duke Richard I of Normandy and after the Viking invasion of 1013, Edward had found refuge at the Norman court. Furthermore, a Norman duke with an interest in the English throne was a useful counter to the continuing menace from Scandinavia. All depended, however, on the attitude of the English earls. In practice, this came to mean what was acceptable to the Godwin family: after the return from exile of Earl Godwin and his sons in 1052, it steadily grew in power soon controlling Northumbria, East Anglia, the southeastern shires as well as Wessex. Earl Harold, who succeeded his father in 1053, had much to lose from an unfavourable change of dynasty and it is not very surprising that, given his military resources and the lack of any clear or accepted procedure to determine the succession, he decided to resist William's claim. It would appear that after failing to bring about a permanent settlement between William and Harold in 1064 or 1065, King Edward belatedly acknowledged the realities of domestic politics and nominated Harold Godwinson his successor.

The main part of this unit is concerned with the contemporary evidence relating to Earl Harold's and Duke William's claims to succeed King Edward and there are concluding sections on Harold's accession and reign. While inconclusive, the issues concerning the English succession in 1066 are far better documented than in any of the previous succession disputes. Since 975 five of the eight reigning kings, including Edward the Confessor, were faced with rival claimants. The relative wealth of documentation on the lead up to 1066 partly reflects the Norman attempt to prove that William was not only the Conqueror but also the rightful heir to the throne. If this could be established then the new king could more easily win the support of both the Church and his subjects, at the same time weakening the moral position of rivals and leaders of resistance. The Norman sources for this period must be viewed within this context.

Further Reading

The problems surrounding the succession are well summarised in Chapter 10 of F. Barlow, *Edward the Confessor* (London, Methuen, 1970) and in Chapters 7 and 8 of D. C. Douglas, *William the Conqueror* (London, Eyre and Spottiswoode, 1964).

1 Edward the Confessor's nomination of Duke William as his heir in 1051

(a) Edward, king of the English, being, according to the dispensation of God, without an heir, sent Robert, Archbishop of Canterbury, to the duke with a message appointing the duke as heir to the kingdom which God had entrusted to him.

> William of Jumièges, *Gesta Normannorum Ducum*, trans. in *English Historical Documents II 1042–1189* (2nd edn, London, Eyre and Spottiswoode 1981), p 228

5 (b) 1051 . . . Then soon came duke William from beyond the sea with a great retinue of Frenchmen, and the king received him and as many of his companions as it pleased him and let him go again.

> Worcester version (D) of *The Anglo-Saxon Chronicle*, trans. G. N. Garmonsway (London, Dent, 1953), p 176

(c) 1051 . . . In this year in spring king Edward appointed Robert . . . Archbishop of Canterbury; and in the same spring he went to
10 Rome for his pallium . . . Then the archbishop returned from Rome . . . and at once went to the king.

> Peterborough version (E) of *The Anglo-Saxon Chronicle*, trans. G. N. Garmonsway (London, Dent, 1953), pp 171–2

Questions

a Accepting both the English and Norman writings as true but incomplete, how can we restructure the events of 1051 and explain the omissions?

★ b What new but temporary conditions enabled Edward to attempt a settlement of the English succession in 1051?

★ c To what extent did Edward the Confessor's patronage policy from 1042 anticipate the Norman alliance of 1051?

2 Harold's visit to William in 1064/5

(a) He (Edward the Confessor) . . . sent to the duke, Harold the greatest of all the counts in his kingdom alike in riches and honour and power. This he did in order that Harold might guarantee the crown to the duke by his fealty and confirm the same with an oath
5 according to Christian usage. When Harold set out on his mission he was borne along by the wind until he reached Ponthieu, and there he fell into the hands of Guy, count of Abbeville, who straightway threw him with his retinue into prison. When the duke heard of this he sent messengers, and by force caused him to be released. Harold
10 thereupon tarried with the duke for some time, and performed fealty to him in respect of the kingdom with many oaths. After this the duke sent him back to the king with many gifts.

William of Jumièges, *Gesta Normannorum Ducum*, trans. in *English Historical Documents II 1042–1189* (2nd edn, London, Eyre and Spottiswoode, 1981), pp 228–9

(b) . . . Edward, king of the English, who loved William as a brother or a son, established him as his heir with a stronger pledge
15 than ever before. The king, who in his holy life showed his desire for a celestial kingdom, felt the hour of his death approaching, and wished to anticipate its inevitable consequences. He therefore dispatched Harold to William in order that he might confirm his promise by an oath. This Harold was of all the king's subjects the
20 richest and the most exalted in honour and power, and his brother and his cousins had previously been offered as hostages in respect of the same succession. The king, indeed, here acted with great prudence in choosing Harold for this task, in the hope that the riches and the authority of this magnate might check disturbance
25 throughout England if the people with their accustomed perfidy should be disposed to overturn what had been determined. Whilst travelling upon this errand Harold only escaped the perils of the sea by making a forced landing on the coast of Ponthieu where he fell into the hands of Count Guy, who threw him and his companions
30 into prison. He might well have thought this a greater misfortune than shipwreck, since among many peoples of the Gauls there was an

abominable custom utterly contrary to Christian charity, whereby, when the powerful and rich were captured, they were thrown ignominiously into prison, and there maltreated and tortured even
35 to the point of death, and afterwards sold as slaves to some magnate. When Duke William heard what had happened he sent messengers at speed, and by prayers and threats he brought about Harold's honourable release. As a result Guy in person conducted his prisoner to the castle of Eu, although he could at his pleasure have tortured or
40 killed him, or sold him into slavery. Since moreover, he did this very honourably without the compulsion of force or bribes, William in gratitude bestowed upon him rich gifts of land and money, and then took Harold with proper honour to Rouen.

This was the chief city of the Norman duchy, and there William
45 sumptuously refreshed Harold with splendid hospitality after all the hardships of his journey. For the duke rejoiced to have so illustrious a guest in a man who had been sent by the nearest and dearest of his friends: one, moreover, who was in England second only to the king, and who might prove a faithful mediator between him and the
50 English. When they had come together in conference at Bonneville, Harold in that place swore fealty to the duke employing the sacred ritual recognised among Christian men. And as is testified by the most truthful and most honourable men who were there present, he took an oath of his own free will in the following terms: firstly that
55 he would be the representative of Duke William at the court of his lord, King Edward, as long as the king lived; secondly that he would employ all his influence and wealth to ensure that after the death of King Edward the kingdom of England should be confirmed in the possession of the duke; thirdly that he would place a garrison of the
60 duke's knights in the castle of Dover and maintain these at his own care and cost; fourthly that in other parts of England at the pleasure of the duke he would maintain garrisons in other castles and make complete provision for their sustenance. The duke on his part who before the oath was taken had received ceremonial homage from
65 him, confirmed to him at his request all his lands and dignities.

William of Poitiers, *Gesta Willelmi ducis Normannorum et regis Anglorum*, trans. in *English Historical Documents II 1042–1189* (2nd edn, London, Eyre and Spottiswoode, 1981), pp 231–2

(d) Harold . . . asked leave of the King to go to Normandy to set free his brother and his nephew who were being held there as hostages . . . The King said to him: 'I will have no part in this; but, not to give the impression of wishing to hinder you, I give you leave
70 to go where you will and to see what you can do. But I have a presentiment that you will only succeed in bringing misfortune upon the whole kingdom and discredit upon yourself. For I know that the Duke is not so simple as to be at all inclined to give them up

(c)

Plate XXV   Here William gave arms to Harold

Plate XXVI   Here William came to Bayeux

Plate XXVII   And Harold made an oath to William

to you unless he foresees that in doing so he will secure some great
75 advantage to himself.' Harold . . . embarked on board ship taking
with him his richest and most honourable men, equipped with a
lordly provision of gold, silver and costly raiment . . . the sea grew
stormy . . . the ship . . . was driven . . . into a river of Ponthieu . . .
Harold was held a prisoner . . . The Duke (William of Normandy)
80 . . . sent messengers to the Lord of Ponthieu and told him that . . .
Harold and his men must be sent to him as quickly as possible . . .

When William had been told why Harold had set out from
England, he replied that his mission would certainly be successful or
it would be his own fault if it was not . . . He said that King Edward,
85 when years before he was detained with him in Normandy . . . had
promised him . . . that if he, Edward, should ever be King of
England, he would make over to William the right to succeed him on
the throne as his heir. William went on to say this: 'If you on your
side undertake to support me in this project and further promise that
90 you will make a stronghold at Dover with a well of water for my use
and that you will at a time agreed between us send your sister to me
that I may give her in marriage to one of my nobles and that you will
take my daughter to be your wife, then I will let you have your
nephew now at once, and your brother safe and sound when I come
95 to England to be King . . .' Then Harold perceived here was danger
whatever way he turned. He could not see any way to escape
without agreeing to all that William wished. So he agreed. Then
William, to ensure that all should thenceforth stand firmly ratified,
had relics of saints brought out and made Harold swear over them.
*Eadmer's History of Recent Events in England: Historia Novorum
in Anglia*, trans. G. Bosanquet (London, The Cresset Press,
1964), pp 6–8

100 (e) When his father had died . . . Harold, pitying the hostages, was
desirous to cross over into Normandy, to bring them home. So he
went to take leave of the King. But Edward strictly forbade him, and
charged and conjured him not to go to Normandy, nor to speak with
duke William; for he might soon be drawn into some snare, as the
105 duke was very shrewd . . . But another book tells me that the King
ordered him to go, for the purpose of assuring duke William, his
cousin, that he should have the realm after his death. How the matter
really was I never knew, and I find it written both the one way and
the other.
110 . . . He made ready two ships, and took the sea at Bodeham
(Bosham) . . . he missed the right course, and touched the coast of
Pontif, where he could neither get away, nor conceal himself . . .
Harold contrived to send off a message privily to the duke William in
Normandy, and told him of his journey . . . the duke . . . got

115 possession of him, and gave in return to the count Guy a fair manor
lying along the river Alne.

William entertained Harold many days in great honour, as was his
due. He took him to many rich tournaments, arrayed him nobly,
gave him horses and arms, and led with him into Brittany – I am not
120 certain whether three or four times – when he had to fight with the
Bretons. And in the meantime he bespoke Harold so fairly, that he
agreed to deliver up England to him, as soon as Edward should die;
and he was to have Ele, one of William's daughters for his wife if he
would, and to swear to all if required, William also binding himself
125 to those terms.

To receive the oath, he caused a parliament to be called. It is
commonly said that it was at Bayeux that he had his great council
assembled. He sent for all the holy bodies thither, and put so many of
them together as to fill a whole chest, and then covered them with a
130 pall; but Harold neither saw them, nor knew of their being there; for
naught was shewn or told to him about it . . . . When Harold placed
his hand upon it, the hand trembled, and the flesh quivered; but he
swore . . . and when Harold had kissed the saints, and had risen
upon his feet, the duke led him up to the chest, and made him stand
135 near it; and took off the chest the pall that had covered it and shewed
Harold upon what holy relics he had sworn; and he was sorely
alarmed at the sight.

Wace's Chronicle of the Norman Conquest from the Roman de Rou,
trans. E. Taylor (London, Pickering, 1837), pp 76–86

Questions

a Why, according to extracts *a* and *b*, does King Edward choose
Harold to visit William in order to guarantee the Norman
succession?

b Why does William of Poitiers in extract *b* stress the dangers that
threatened Harold while imprisoned in Ponthieu (lines 30–35)?

c Explain what is meant by the 'inevitable consequences' of King
Edward's death in extract *b* (line 17).

★ d What reason had King Edward to love William 'as a brother or a
son' (lines 13–14)?

e What factual difference is there between the tapestry captions in
extract *c* and William of Poitiers' account in extract *b*?

f How do the writers of extracts *d* and *e* alter the role of King
Edward in Harold's mission as established by the first two
extracts?

g In what ways does the nature of the bargain struck between
Harold and William differ between extracts *b*, *d* and *e*?

h Wace, the author of extract *e*, was writing in the twelfth century.
Can his account have any value for historians?

3 Edward the Confessor's deathbed nomination of Harold as his successor

(a) Harold's envoy addressing Duke William and the Norman magnates before the battle of Hastings, followed by William's apostrophe to the dead Harold.

He certainly remembers that King Edward long ago decided that you would be his heir, and that he himself in Normandy gave surety to you concerning that succession. Nevertheless, he knows that this kingdom is his by right, as granted to him by gift of that same king
5   his lord upon his deathbed. For since the time when the blessed Augustine came into England it has been the common custom of this nation that a gift made at the point of death is held as valid . . . Your last hours show with what right you were elevated to the kingship by the grant of Edward on his deathbed.

William of Poitiers, *Gesta Willelmi ducis Normannorum et regis Anglorum*, trans. Allen R. Brown, *The Norman Conquest* (London, Edward Arnold, 1984), pp 30 and 36

10 (c) Edward the noble protected his fatherland,
His realm and people: until suddenly came
That bitter death, which took so cruelly
The prince from the earth. Angels bore his
Righteous soul within Heaven's light.
15   Yet did the wise king entrust his kingdom
To a man of high rank, to Harold himself.
The noble earl, who ever
Faithfully obeyed his noble lord
In words and deeds, neglecting nothing
20   Whereof the national king stood in need.

Abingdon version (C) of *The Anglo-Saxon Chronicle*, trans. G. N. Garmonsway (London, Dent, 1953), p 194

(d) Archbishop Stigund . . . whispered in the ear of the earl that the king was broken with age and disease and knew not what he said . . . when he (King Edward) was sick into death . . . he addressed his last words to the queen . . . 'May God be gracious to this my wife for the
25 zealous solicitude of her service . . .' And stretching forth his hand to his governor, her brother, Harold, he said, 'I commend this woman and all the kingdom to your protection. Serve and honour her with faithful obedience as your lady and sister, which she is, and do not despoil her, as long as she lives, of any due honour got from
30 me.
Likewise I also commend those men who have left their native land for love of me, and have up till now served me faithfully. Take from them an oath of fealty, if they should so wish, and protect and retain them, or send them with your safe conduct safely across the

(b) Plate XXXII   Here King Edward in bed speaks to his liegemen

The Bayeux Tapestry. Figures surrounding the dying king from left to right: Queen Edith, Harold, Archbishop Stigund and Robert Fitzwimarch

35 Channel to their own homes with all that they have acquired in my
service . . . I ask that you do not conceal my death, but announce it
promptly in all parts, so that all the faithful can beseech the mercy of
Almighty God on me, a sinner.'
    Vita Ædwardi Regis (The Life of King Edward), ed. and trans.
    Frank Barlow (London, Nelson, 1962), pp 76 and 79–80

Questions

a   How convincing is the Norman evidence in extracts *a* and *b* that
    Edward finally nominated Harold as his successor?
b   Is the evidence regarding the bequest of the kingdom to Harold
    in extract *d* any more or less ambiguous than that in extract *c*?
c   What argument was open to the Norman writers to invalidate
    the deathbed nomination?

4   Harold's accession to the English throne

(a) . . . There came the unwelcome report that the land of England
had lost its king, and that Harold had been crowned in his stead. This
insensate Englishman did not wait for the public choice, but
breaking his oath, and with the support of a few ill-disposed
5 partisans, he seized the throne of the best of kings on the very day of
his funeral, and when all the people were bewailing their loss. He
was ordained king by the unhallowed consecration of Stigund who
had justly been deprived of his priesthood by the zeal and anathema
of the apostolic see.
    William of Poitiers, *Gesta Willelmi ducis Normannorum et regis
    Anglorum*, trans. in *English Historical Documents II 1042–1189*
    (2nd edn, London, Eyre and Spottiswoode, 1981), p 232

10 (b) Soon afterwards King Edward . . . died at London and was
buried in the new minster which he had founded to the west of the
city, and had had dedicated only the week before . . . There on the
day of the funeral, whilst the crowds watched the last rites of their
beloved king with streaming eyes, Harold had himself consecrated
15 by Archbishop Stigund alone, whom the pope had suspended from
divine service for various misdeeds, without the common consent of
the other bishops, earls and nobles, and so by stealth stole the glory
of the crown and royal purple. When the English learned of Harold's
presumptuous usurpation, they were moved to anger; some of the
20 most powerful were ready to resist him by force and refused to
submit to him in any way. Others, however, not knowing how to
escape his tyranny which daily grew worse, and considering too that
they were powerless either to depose him or to establish another
king to profit the kingdom whilst he was in power, bowed their
25 necks to his yoke and so increased his power for evil. In a short time

the kingdom which he had nefariously seized was polluted with crimes too horrible to relate.

> *The Ecclesiastical History of Orderic Vitalis*, ed. Marjorie Chibnall (Oxford, O.U.P., 1969), vol II, pp 137–9

(c) 1066. On Thursday the vigil of our Lord's Epiphany, in the Fourth Indiction, the pride of the English, the pacific king, Edward,
30 son of king Ethelred, died at London, having reigned over the English twenty-three years six months and seven days. The next day he was buried in kingly style amid the bitter lamentations of all present. After his burial the under-king, Harold, son of Earl Godwine, whom the king had nominated as his successor, was
35 chosen king by the chief magnates of all England; and on the same day Harold was crowned with great ceremony by Aldred, archbishop of York.

> '*Florence of Worcester*', trans. in *English Historical Documents II 1042–1189* (2nd edn, London, Eyre and Spottiswoode, 1981), p 225

(d) In this year (1065) the abbey church at Westminster was consecrated on Holy Innocents' day (28 December) and king
40 Edward passed away on the vigil of, and was buried on, Epiphany (6 January) in the newly consecrated abbey church of Westminster. Earl Harold succeeded to the kingdom of England as the king granted it to him and he was elected thereto. He was consecrated king on Epiphany.

> Peterborough version (E) of *The Anglo-Saxon Chronicle*, trans. G. N. Garmonsway (London, Dent, 1953), pp 195 and 197

Questions

a In what ways does the second extract show a hardening of the anti-Harold legend established by the first extract?
b How does Florence of Worcester demonstrate his pro-Godwinist position in extract *c*?
c What are the main differences of fact between the four accounts of Harold's accession?
★ d What were the 'various misdeeds' (line 16) for which Stigund had been excommunicated?
★ e What factors would have encouraged a speedy settlement of the English succession in January 1066?

5 'Florence of Worcester's account of the reign of King Harold Godwinson

(a) . . . Harold immediately began to abolish unjust laws and to make good ones; to patronize churches and monasteries; to pay particular reverence to bishops, abbots, monks and clerks; and to show himself pious, humble and affable to all good men. But he 5 treated malefactors with great severity, and gave general orders to his earls, ealdormen, sheriffs and thegns to imprison all thieves, robbers and disturbers of the kingdom. He laboured in his own person by sea and by land for the protection of his realm. On 24 April . . . a comet was seen . . . Shortly afterwards Earl Tosti . . . landed 10 in the Isle of Wight. After making the islanders pay tribute he departed and went pillaging along the sea-coast until he came to Sandwich. As soon as King Harold who was then at London heard this, he assembled a large fleet and a contingent of horsemen, and prepared himself to go to Sandwich. Tosti, learning of this, took 15 some of the shipmen of that place . . . and set his course towards Lindsey, where he burnt many villages and put many men to death. Thereupon, Edwin, earl of the Mercians, and Morcar, earl of the Northumbrians, hastened up with an army and expelled them from that part of the country. Afterwards he went to Malcolm, king of 20 Scots . . . Meanwhile, King Harold arrived at Sandwich and waited there for his fleet. When it was assembled, he crossed over with it to the Isle of Wight, and, inasmuch as William count of the Normans, was preparing to invade England with an army, he watched all the summer and autumn for his coming. In addition he distributed a land 25 force at suitable points along the sea-coast. But about (8 September) provisions fell short so that the naval and land forces returned home. After this Harold Hardraada, king of the Norwegians . . . arrived on a sudden at the mouth of the river Tyne with a powerful fleet of more than five hundred large ships. Earl Tosti, according to a previous 30 arrangement, joined him with his fleet. Hastening, they entered the Humber and sailing up the Ouse against the stream landed at Riccall. On hearing this, king Harold marched with speed towards Northumbria. But before his arrival the two brother-earls, Edwin and Morcar, at the head of a large army fought a battle with the 35 Norwegians on the northern banks of the river Ouse near York on Wednesday . . . (20 September). They fought so bravely at the onset that many of the enemy were overthrown; but after a long contest the English were unable to withstand the attacks of the Norwegians and fled with great loss. More were drowned in the river than slain 40 on the field . . . Five days after this . . . as Harold, king of the English, was coming to York with many thousand well-armed fighting men, he fell in with the Norwegians at a place called Stamford Bridge. He slew King Harold (Hardraada) and Earl Tosti with the greater part of their army and gained a complete victory. 45 Nevertheless the battle was stoutly contested. Harold . . . permitted Olaf, the son of the Norwegian king, and Paul, earl of Orkney . . . to return home unmolested with twenty ships and the survivors, but only after they had sworn oaths of submission and had given hostages.

'Florence of Worcester', trans. in *English Historical Documents II 1042–1189* (2nd edn, London, Eyre and Spottiswoode, 1981), pp 225–7

Questions

a How far does Florence of Worcester's account support his statement that King Harold 'laboured in his own person by sea and by land for the protection of his realm' (lines 7–8)?

* *b* Why did Harald Hardraada wait until September 1066 before invading England?

II Conquest and Consolidation

Introduction

Duke William began preparing for the conquest of England after receiving news of Harold's coronation in January 1066. He secured the support of his leading vassals, appealed for papal approval and ordered the construction of an invasion fleet. Steps were also taken to ensure the proper administration of Normandy in his absence with power devolving upon the Duchess Matilda and their eldest son Robert. Before mid-August, the ships were ready and William was assembling his army which finally numbered around 7000 men. Adverse winds or deliberate delaying tactics by the Normans prevented an embarkation before late September by which time King Harold was in York having defeated Hardraada and Tostig at Stamford Bridge. The strategy of rapid troop movement followed by surprise attack, though stunningly successful against the Norwegians failed to confound Duke William and it was, by some accounts, the Normans who took the English by surprise at Hastings.

While this famous battle eliminated the most dangerous and powerful elements of the Godwin family, together with other unnamed English magnates, it did not constitute a conquest. Edwin and Morcar, the brother earls of Mercia and Northumbria, Waltheof, the son of Siward, and Edgar Aetheling were all still at large and capable of leading resistance to the Norman claim. London had yet to fall and rebellion, lawlessness and further invasion were all but assured. The Conquest was necessarily a prolonged and painful operation, always open to challenge and dependent for its survival upon a number of swift, decisive military actions against areas of disaffection. If, in retrospect, the Conqueror's crown appeared secure from the start, that is only a tribute to his energetic determination to preserve the new dynasty.

This chapter begins with three of the earliest classic accounts of the Battle of Hastings which, despite the cursory descriptions in the English sources, remains one of the best recorded battles of the earlier middle ages. Guy of Amiens' narrative must be treated with caution, however, as it is now thought to be a mere literary exercise composed in the twelfth century. The joint Danish and northern challenge of 1069/1070 provides the first major threat to William's position and the seriousness with which he regarded the events of those years can be inferred from the ruthlessness of his response. By contrast, the revolt of the earls, though potentially dangerous, failed to gain momentum and the punishments meted out to the offending parties were far more selective than the apparently indiscriminate slaughter of the 'harrying of the north'.

Further Reading

The Battle of Hastings is discussed at length in J. F. C. Fuller, *The Decisive Battles of the Western World* (London, Eyre and Spottiswoode, 1954), vol I and there is a useful summary in F. M. Stenton, *Anglo-Saxon England* (Oxford, O.U.P., 1943). There are a number of good modern accounts and discussions of the Norman Conquest including R. R. Darlington, *The Norman Conquest* (London University, 1963), H. R. Loyn, *The Norman Conquest* (London, Hutchinson, 1965) and Allen R. Brown, *The Normans and the Norman Conquest* (London, Boydell, 1969).

1 The Battle of Hastings

(a) William, count of the Normans, had arrived with a countless host of horsemen, slingers, archers and foot-soldiers, and had brought with him also powerful help from all parts of Gaul. It was reported that he had landed at Pevensey. Therefore the king at once,
5 and in great haste, marched with his army to London. Although he well knew that some of the bravest Englishmen had fallen in the two former battles, and that one half of his army had not yet arrived, he did not hesitate to advance with all speed into Sussex against his enemies. On Saturday, 22 October, (mistake for 14 October) before
10 a third of his army was in order for fighting, he joined battle with them nine miles from Hastings, where his foes had erected a castle. But in as much as the English were drawn up in a narrow place, many retired from the ranks, and very few remained true to him. Nevertheless from the third hour of the day until dusk, he bravely
15 withstood the enemy, and fought so valiantly and stubbornly in his defence that the enemy's forces could make hardly any impression. At last, after great slaughter on both sides, about twilight the king, alas, fell. There were slain also Earl Gyrth, and his brother, Earl Leofwine, and nearly all the magnates of England . . . Harold
20 reigned nine months and as many days. On hearing of his death Earls Edwin and Morcar, who had withdrawn themselves from the conflict, went to London . . . and . . . with the citizens of London and the shipmen planned to elevate to the throne Prince Edgar . . . and promised they would renew the contest under his command.
25 But while many were preparing to go to the fight, the earls withdrew their assistance and returned home with their army.

'Florence of Worcester', trans. in *English Historical Documents II 1042–1189* (2nd edn, Eyre and Spottiswoode, 1981), p 227

(b) He then advanced in good order with the papal banner which had been granted to him borne aloft at the head of his troops. In the van he placed foot-soldiers equipped with arrows and crossbows; in
30 the second rank came the more heavily armed infantry clad in hauberks; and finally came the squadrons of knights in the midst of whom he rode himself showing invincible courage and in such a position that he could give his orders by hand or by voice . . . From all the provinces of the English a vast host had gathered together . . .
35 all were inspired by the love of their country which they desired, however unjustly, to defend against foreigners. The land of the Danes who were allied to them had also sent copious reinforcements . . . They took up their position on higher ground, on a hill abutting the forest through which they had just come. There, at once
40 dismounting from their horses, they drew themselves up on foot and in very close order. The duke and his men in no way dismayed by the difficulty of the ground came slowly up the hill, and the terrible sound of trumpets on both sides signalled the beginning of the battle . . . the Norman foot drawing nearer provoked the English by
45 raining death and wounds upon them with their missiles. But the English resisted valiantly . . . and they hurled back spears and javelins and weapons of all kinds together with axes and stones fastened to pieces of wood . . . The knights came after the chief, being in the nearmost rank, and all disdaining to fight at long range
50 were eager to use their swords. The shouts both of the Normans and of the barbarians were drowned in the clash of arms and by the cries of the dying, and for a long time the battle raged with the utmost fury. The English, however, had the advantage of the ground and profited by remaining within their position in close order. They
55 gained further superiority from their numbers, from the impregnable front which they preserved, and most of all from the manner in which their weapons found easy passage through the shields and armour of their enemies.

Thus they bravely withstood and successfully repulsed those who
60 were engaging them at close quarters, and inflicted loss upon the men who were shooting missiles at them from a distance. Then the foot-soldiers and the Breton knights, panic-stricken by the violence of the assault, broke in flight before the English and also the auxiliary troops on the left wing, and the whole army of the duke was in
65 danger of retreat . . . the Normans believed that their duke and lord was killed . . .

Seeing a large part of the hostile host pursuing his own troops, the prince thrust himself in front of those in flight, shouting at them and threatening them with his spear. Staying their retreat, he took off his
70 helmet, and standing before them bareheaded he cried 'Look at me well. I am still alive and by the grace of God I shall yet prove victor . . .' With these words he restored their courage, and, leaping to the front and wielding his death-dealing sword, he defied the

enemy who merited death for their disloyalty to him their prince.
75 Inflamed by his ardour, the Normans then surrounded several
thousands of their pursuers and rapidly cut them down so that not
one escaped. Heartened by their success, they then furiously carried
their attack to the main body of the English host, which even after
their losses scarcely seemed diminished in number. The English
80 fought confidently with all their strength, striving in particular to
prevent the attackers from penetrating within their ranks, which
indeed were so closely massed together that even the dead had not
space in which to fall . . .

Realising that they could not without severe loss overcome an
85 army massed so strongly in close formation, the Normans and their
allies feigned flight and simulated a retreat . . . The barbarians
thinking victory within their grasp shouted with triumph, and
heaping insults upon our men, threatened utterly to destroy them.
Several thousand of them, as before, gave rapid pursuit to those
90 whom they thought to be in flight; but the Normans suddenly
wheeling their horses surrounded them and cut down their pursuers
so that not one was left alive. Twice was this ruse employed with the
utmost success, and then they attacked those that remained with
redoubled fury . . . At last the English began to weary, and as if
95 confessing their crime in their defeat they submitted to their
punishment . . .

Duke William . . . dominated this battle, checking his own men in
flight, strengthening their spirit, and sharing their dangers . . .
Thrice his horse fell under him; thrice he leapt upon the ground; and
100 thrice he quickly avenged the death of his steed . . .

Evening was now falling . . . the English . . . knew they had lost a
great part of their army, and they also knew that their king with two
of his brothers and many of their greatest men had fallen. Those who
remained were almost exhausted . . . Dismayed at the implacable
105 bearing of the duke . . . they began to fly as swiftly as they could,
some on foot, some along the roads, but most over the trackless
country . . . The Normans eagerly carried on the pursuit, and
striking the rebels in the back brought a happy end to this famous
victory.

William of Poitiers, *Gesta Willelmi ducis Normannorum et regis
Anglorum*, trans. in *English Historical Documents II 1042– 1189*
(2nd edn, London, Eyre and Spottiswoode, 1981), pp 239–43

110 (c) He (William) dispatched the foot in advance to open the battle
with arrows, and set crossbowmen in the midst so that their
speeding shafts might pierce the faces of the English . . .

Preparing to meet the enemy, the king mounted the hill and
strengthened both his wings with noblemen. On the highest point of
115 the summit he planted his banner, and ordered his other standards to
be set up. All the men dismounted and left their horses in the rear,

and taking their stand on foot they let the trumpets sound for battle.

The humble and God-fearing duke led a more measured advance and courageously approached the steeps of the hill. The foot-soldiers ran ahead to engage the enemy with arrows . . . The helmeted warriors hastened to close ranks; on both sides the foemen raged with brandished spears . . .

. . . while the battle hung in ominous suspense . . . a player . . . rode out before the countless army of the duke. He heartened the men of France and terrified the English, and, tossing his sword high, he sported with it. A certain Englishman . . . was fired with the ardour proper to a soldier's heart – heedless of life, he sprang forward to meet his death. The mummer, surnamed Taillefer . . . pierced the Englishman's shield with his keen lance and hewed the head from the prostrate body with his sword . . .

Now the French attacked the left, the Bretons the right, the duke with the Normans fought in the centre. The English stood firm on their ground in the closest order . . . bodies could not be laid down, nor did the dead give place to living soldiers . . .

The French, versed in strategems, skilled in warfare, pretended to fly as if defeated. The English peasantry rejoiced and believed they had won; they pursued in the rear with naked swords . . . But those who feigned flight wheeled on the pursuers . . . ten thousand suffered destruction in that place . . . But the very powerful force that survived in the battle attacked more furiously and counted their losses nothing. The English people, prevailing by their number, repulsed the enemy and by their might compelled him to turn – and then the flight which had first been a ruse became enforced by valour. The Normans fled, their shields covered their backs!

When the duke saw his people retreat vanquished, he rushed to confront the rout . . . Raging, he himself bared his head of the helmet. To the Normans he showed a furious countenance – to the French he spoke words of entreaty . . . their faces grew red with shame. They wheeled, they turned to face the enemy. The duke, as leader, was the first to strike; after him the rest laid on. Coming to their senses, they regained strength by scorning fear . . .

Harold's brother, Gyrth . . . poising a javelin, he hurled it . . . The flying weapon wounded the body of the horse and forced the duke to fight on foot . . . he rushed upon the young man . . . Hewing him limb from limb . . .

When the duke was horsed, he then assailed the enemy more strongly . . . as he dyed the field with the blood of the slain, the son of Helloc . . . lay . . . meaning to kill him. But when the javelin was cast, the horse received the blow . . . the duke . . . was stunned to have been robbed of two horses in a single encounter . . . Seeing the author of the crime lurking at a distance in the press, he rushed forthwith to destroy him . . .

Now the victor, joyful France almost ruled the field . . . the duke

sighted the king far off on the steeps of the hill . . . He called Eustace
165 to him . . . Hugh, the noble heir of Ponthieu, escorted these two . . .
fourth was Giffard . . . these four bore arms for the destruction of
the king . . . The first, cleaving his breast through the shield with his
point, drenched the earth with a gushing torrent of blood; the second
smote off his head below the protection of his helmet and the third
170 pierced the inwards of his belly with his lance; the fourth hewed off
his thigh and bore away the severed limb . . .
   The flying rumour 'Harold is dead!' spread through the fray . . .
The English refused battle. Vanquished they besought mercy;
despairing of life, they fled from death. Two thousand in number the
175 duke sent to Hades then, not counting the other thousands beyond
telling. It was evening; already the wheeling heavens were turning
day to twilight when God made the duke the victor.
        The Carmen de Hastingae Proelio of Guy, Bishop of Amiens, eds
        C. Morton and H. Muntz (Oxford, Clarendon Press, 1972),
        pp 23–37

Questions

a What reasons does the first extract provide for King Harold's
   defeat at Hastings?
b According to extract *b*, early on in the battle 'the whole army of
   the duke was in danger of retreat' (lines 64–5). What enabled the
   English to gain the initial advantage at Hastings?
c How does extract *c* differ from extract *b* in its identification of the
   circumstances leading up to the threatened rout of the Norman
   army?
d The *Carmen* reports that 'Two thousand in number the duke sent
   to Hades . . . not counting the other thousands beyond telling'
   (lines 174–6). Discounting the obvious exaggerations, what do
   extracts *b* and *c* reveal about William's personal contribution to
   the battle?
e In view of the claim by some historians that the *Carmen* is a mere
   literary exercise based on William of Poitiers' account, what
   episodes reported in extract *c* should be regarded with particular
   scepticism?
f Florence of Worcester announced that William 'arrived with a
   countless host of horsemen, slingers, archers and foot-soldiers'
   together with 'powerful help from all parts of Gaul' (lines 1–3).
   How, according to the succeeding extracts, were these troops
   deployed on the battlefield and what information is given about
   the composition and weaponry of King Harold's army?

2 1069/1070: The Danish invasion and northern revolt

(a) At this time Swein king of Denmark fitted out a great fleet of
Danes and English; and giving the command to his two sons,

Osbern his brother, two bishops and three earls whom he held in high esteem, sent it to England. He had received many messengers from the English begging for help and sending subsidies; and he was moved by the death and disaster that had overtaken his men in Harold's war; but he was influenced even more by his desire for the kingdom to which, as nephew of King Edward and son of Hardacnut, he had a claim of inheritance . . . The moment he (King William) heard of the coming of the Danes he sent a messenger to York to tell his men to prepare for an attack and send for him if they were hard-pressed. The custodians of the castles there replied that they could hold out without help for a year. But already the Aetheling, Waltheof, Siward, and the other English leaders had joined the Danes.

. . . The Danes reached York, and a general rising of the inhabitants swelled their ranks . . . The garrison made a rash sally to attack them and engaged them ill-advisedly within the city walls. Unable to resist such numbers they were all slain or taken prisoner. The castles were left undefended.

. . . About this time the West Saxons of Dorset and Somerset with their neighbours attacked Montacute, but by the will of God failed to take it. For the men of Winchester, London, and Salisbury, under the leadership of Geoffrey bishop of Coutances, marched against them, killed some, captured and mutilated others, and put the rest to flight. The Welshmen and men of Chester besieged the royal stronghold at Shrewsbury, and were assisted by the native citizens, the powerful and warlike Edric the Wild, and other untameable Englishmen. The men of Devon were attacking Exeter in the same way, allied with the hordes from Cornwall . . .

Meanwhile the king had had no difficulty in crushing large forces of rebels at Stafford. In all these battles much blood had flowed on both sides, and combatants and non-combatants alike had been reduced to great wretchedness by the disturbances . . . So at last they (the royal forces) approached York only to learn that the Danes had fled. The king assigned officers and castellans with armed retainers to repair the castles in the city, and left others on the bank of the Humber to ward off the Danes. He himself continued to comb forests and remote mountainous places, stopping at nothing to hunt out the enemy hidden there. His camps were spread out over an area of a hundred miles. He cut down many in his vengeance; destroyed the lairs of others; harried the land, and burned homes to ashes. Nowhere else had William shown such cruelty. Shamefully he succumbed to this vice, for he made no effort to restrain his fury and punished the innocent with the guilty. In his anger he commanded that all crops and herds, chattels and food of every kind should be brought together and burned to ashes with consuming fire, so that the whole region north of Humber might be stripped of all means of sustenance. In consequence so serious a scarcity was felt in England,

50 and so terrible a famine fell upon the humble and defenceless populace, that more than 100,000 Christian folk of both sexes, young and old alike, perished of hunger. My narrative has frequently had occasion to praise William, but for this act which condemned the innocent and guilty alike to die by slow starvation I

55 cannot commend him. For when I think of helpless children, young men in the prime of life, and hoary greybeards perishing alike of hunger I am so moved to pity that I would rather lament the griefs and sufferings of the wretched people than make a vain attempt to flatter the perpetrator of such infamy. Moreover, I declare that

60 assuredly such brutal slaughter cannot remain unpunished. For the almighty Judge watches over high and low alike; he will weigh the deeds of all men in a fair balance, and as a just avenger will punish wrongdoing, as the eternal law makes clear to all men.

The Ecclesiastical History of Orderic Vitalis, ed. Marjorie Chibnall (6 vols, Oxford, O.U.P., 1969–80), vol II, pp 225–33

(b) Soon thereafter (1069) three sons of king Swein with two

65 hundred and forty ships came from Denmark into the Humber, and with them jarl Osbern and jarl Thurkil. There they were met by prince Edgar, earl Waltheof, Maerleswein, earl Gospatric with the Northumbrians, and all the people of the country. Forming an immense host, riding and marching in high spirits, they all

70 resolutely advanced on York and stormed and destroyed the castle, seizing innumerable treasures therein, slaying many hundreds of Frenchmen and carrying off great numbers to their ships. Before the shipmen had come thither, the French had burnt the borough to the ground, and had completely laid waste and burnt down the sacred

75 church of St. Peter. When the king learnt this, he marched northward with all the levies he could muster, and plundered and utterly laid waste that shire. The troops lay all winter in the Humber, where the king could not reach them. The king spent Christmas in York and remained in the north all the winter, returning to

80 Winchester for Easter of that (1070) year. . . . In the same summer the (Danish) troops sailed into the Thames, and lay there two days, and set sail afterwards for Denmark.

Worcester version (D) of *The Anglo-Saxon Chronicle*, trans. G. N. Garmonsway (London, Dent, 1953), pp 204–6

Questions

a   Why, according to the first extract, does King Swein order his 'great fleet' against England? What factual inaccuracy is there in the explanation of his motives?

b   Orderic Vitalis is clearly appalled by William's harsh response to the northern revolt declaring that 'such brutal slaughter cannot remain unpunished' (line 60). How could William have defended his actions based on the evidence in the two extracts?

c What are the main differences in the way the two sources record the events of 1069/70?

3 The Revolt of the Earls 1075

(a) Two powerful English earls, Roger of Hereford and his brother-in-law Ralph of Norwich, plotted together to stir up rebellion, wrest the realm of England from King William, and assume authority – or rather tyranny – over it . . . Considering the
5   changes of fortune and the advantages of the present moment they said to their allies and supporters: 'All thinking men believe that an opportune moment must be seized; and that the brave should set their hands to a great venture when the time is ripe. We have never known a time more apt for winning the realm than that which has
10 now come to us through the grace of God. The man who now calls himself king is unworthy, since he is a bastard, and heaven has made it plain that it is not God's pleasure that such a leader should govern the kingdom. He is harassed on every side by wars overseas; he is attacked as much by his own kin as by strangers, and is deserted by
15 his closest followers in the thick of battle. This is his just desert for his sins, which are all too well known everywhere. For he disinherited William Werlenc, count of Mortain, for a hasty word and drove him out of Normandy; he entertained Walter count of Pontoise, a nephew of King Edward and his wife Biota at Falaise,
20 and murdered both in one night with a poisoned draught. He also poisoned that most valiant count, Conan, a man of such valour that his death cast the whole of Brittany into deep mourning. These and many others are the crimes of William against his kindred and connexions, and he does not hesitate to commit similar evil deeds
25 against us and our peers. He presumptuously invaded the fair kingdom of England and unjustly slew its true heirs or drove them into harsh exile. He did not reward the supporters who raised him above his own people as he ought to have done, but showed ingratitude to many who had shed their blood in his service and on
30 the slightest pretext punished them with death as if they had been enemies. To victors who had endured wounds he gave barren estates, wasted and depopulated by his army; and after they had made these lands fertile he began to covet them, and either took them back or appropriated part of them. All men hate him, and his death
35 would cause great rejoicing. Consider now; the greater part of his army is detained overseas, heavily engaged in continual fighting. The English are concerned only in filling their fields: feasts and convivialities are more to their taste than battles; nevertheless they yearn to see the ruin of their kinsmen avenged.' With these and
40 similar arguments, urging each other to undertake the treachery they

had conceived, the conspirators sought the ear of Waltheof earl of Northampton and tempted him with such reasoning as this: 'See, gallant lord, now is the appointed hour for you to recover your lost fiefs and take just vengeance for the injuries you have suffered. Join
45 our party and stand with us; we can promise you a third part of England . . .'

Waltheof replied: 'In such affairs the greatest caution is necessary; and every man in every country owes absolute loyalty to his liege lord. King William has lawfully received the oath of fealty which I
50 his vassal rightly swore, and has given his niece to me in marriage as a pledge of lasting loyalty. He has given me a rich earldom and counted me amongst his closest friends. How can I be unfaithful to such a lord, unless I utterly desecrate my faith? I am known all over the country, and it would cause great scandal if – which Heaven
55 forbid – I were publicly proclaimed a sacrilegious traitor. No good song is ever sung of a traitor. All peoples brand apostates and traitors as wolves, and consider them worthy of hanging – if they can – condemn them to the gallows with every kind of ignominy and insult . . .
60 When Ralph the Breton and Roger heard these words they were bitterly disappointed and bound him by a terrible oath not to reveal their conspiracy . . .

The Ecclesiastical History of Orderic Vitalis, ed. Marjorie Chibnall (6 vols, Oxford, O.U.P., 1969–80), vol II, pp 311–15

(b) In this year (1075) William gave the daughter of William fitzOsbern in marriage to earl Ralph: this same Ralph was a Breton
65 on his mother's side, and Ralph his father was English, and was born in Norfolk. On this account the king gave his (Ralph's) son the earldom there, and the earldom of Suffolk as well. He then brought his bride to Norwich.

There that bridale
70 Led many to bale.

Earl Roger was present at the wedding, together with earl Waltheof and bishops and abbots, and there they plotted to drive their royal lord from his kingdom. This was soon made known to the king in Normandy. Earl Ralph and earl Roger were the leaders of this plot,
75 and they won over the Bretons to their side, and also sent to Denmark for a pirate host. Roger went west to his earldom and gathered his people together to the king's detriment as he thought, whereas events turned out greatly to their own misfortune. Ralph, too, endeavoured to take the field with people from his earldom, but
80 the garrison of the (Norman) castles which were in England, together with the inhabitants of the country, opposed them and did everything to hinder them, so that nothing was accomplished and

he was glad to escape to his ships. His wife remained behind in the castle, which she held until they made terms with her, whereupon she left England with all her followers who wished to accompany her. The king returned thereafter to England, and seized his kinsman, earl Roger, and imprisoned him. Earl Waltheof went oversea, and confessed his treachery: he asked for pardon and offered treasures, but the king made light of his offence until he returned to England, and then had him arrested.

Soon after this two hundred ships came from Denmark with their leaders Cnut, son of king Swein, and jarl Hakon on board, but they durst not join battle with king William . . . The king spent Christmas at Westminster, and there all the Bretons who attended that bridal at Norwich were sentenced to punishment:

> Some of them were blinded,
> Some of them were banished,
> Some were brought to shame,
> So all traitors to the king
> Were laid low.

Worcester version (D) of *The Anglo-Saxon Chronicle*, trans. G. N. Garmonsway (London, Dent, 1953), pp 210–12

Questions

a   In 1075 Earls Roger and Ralph claim that they 'have never known a time more apt for winning the realm' (lines 8–9). How convincingly do they argue that the present is the ideal time to wrest power from William?

b   Waltheof is offered 'a third part of England' and other prizes if he joins the rebellion. Why does he refuse to become actively involved?

c   In what way does the degree of Waltheof's involvement change between the two accounts?

d   How far does the evidence in extract b support the conspirators' view of William that 'All men hate him, and his death would cause great rejoicing' (lines 34–5)?

III   The English Church and the Norman Conquest

Introduction

After 1066, great changes took place within the English Church and in its relationship to secular authority. Internally, reforms were carried out to remove abuses, diminish corruption and improve the administration of dioceses. Externally, a crisis developed as the papacy began to challenge the royal prerogative in an attempt to ensure the freedom and autonomy of the episcopacy. How far these changes were the result of the Norman Conquest is difficult to establish, for despite the questionable primacy of Stigund, the English Church was not a hopelessly decadent and provincial institution on the eve of William's invasion. In fact, it already contained a number of bishops, some of them foreign, who were in favour of reform, attended conciliar councils abroad and maintained close contact with Rome. Furthermore, the buying and selling of ecclesiastical offices and the marriage and sexual immorality of the clergy were widespread on the continent as well as in England.

Nevertheless, William's accession undoubtedly accelerated the pace of reform as he clearly appreciated the advantages of a strong and efficient national church that could use its influence to buttress his own authority. The working partnership between Lanfranc and William seems to have been satisfactory to both sides as the archbishop was a moderate reformer willing to enlist the help of his king and temporise over the more ambitious papal demands. This harmony between the king and the primate rapidly deteriorated, however, with the appointment of Anselm to Canterbury in 1093. Along with the more extreme reformers Anselm argued that lay control of the church, which was primarily exercised through the king's traditional right to distribute church offices, would have to be removed if the impetus of reform was to be maintained. While the logic of this case was reinforced by William Rufus' mercenary practice of delaying ecclesiastical appointments, it ignored the bishops' important feudal and executive obligations. After much bitter conflict resulting in Anselm's exiles of 1097 and 1103, a compromise was reached at le Bec in 1106, ratified at a council in London during the following year. Henceforth the symbolic investiture with ring and staff was to be performed by the archbishop but the newly elected prelate had to do homage to the king for his lay fief or land held in return for feudal services. In practice, a strong king could still determine the composition of the higher clergy and this agreement formed the basis of Church State relations until the English Reformation.

Further Reading

For a good and readable summary of the English Church under the Normans see the relevant sections in F. Barlow, *The Feudal Kingdom of England 1042–1216* (3rd edn, London, Longman, 1972). More detailed coverage can be found in F. Barlow, *The English Church 1066–1154* (London, Longman, 1979).

1 William and the Church

(a) William, by the grace of God, king of the English, to Ralph Bainard, Geoffrey of Manneville and Peter of Valognes, and to all his other liegemen in Essex, Hertfordshire and Middlesex greeting. Be it known to you and to all my liegemen who are in England that by
5 the common council and counsel of the archbishops, bishops, abbots and of all the magnates of my kingdom, I have ordained that the episcopal laws shall be amended, because before my time these were not properly administered in England according to the precepts of the holy canons. Wherefore I order, and by my royal authority I
10 command, that no bishop or archdeacon shall henceforth hold pleas relating to the episcopal laws in the hundred court; nor shall they bring to the judgement of secular men any matter which concerns the rule of souls; but anyone cited under the episcopal laws in respect of any plea of crime shall come to the place which the bishop shall
15 choose and name, and there he shall plead his case, or answer for his crime. He shall not be tried according to the law of the hundred court, but he shall submit to the justice of God and his bishop in accordance with the canons and the episcopal laws. Moreover, if anyone, puffed up with pride, shall refuse to come to the bishop's
20 court, he shall be summoned three times, and if, after this, he shall still fail to appear, he shall be excommunicated; and if the strength and justice of the king and his sheriff shall be needed to carry this into effect, this support will be forthcoming. Anyone failing to appear at the bishop's court after the summons shall pay the appropriate
25 penalty according to episcopal law. By virtue of my authority I also forbid any sheriff or reeve or official of the king or any layman to interfere with the laws which pertain to the bishop; nor in these cases shall any layman bring another man to justice until the judgement of the bishop has been given. Judgement shall not be given except at the
30 seat of the bishop or in some place that the bishop shall appoint for this purpose.
    Writ of William I, probably dated April 1072, concerning

spiritual and temporal courts, trans. in *English Historical Documents II 1042–1189* (2nd edn, London, Eyre and Spottiswoode, 1981), pp 647–8

(b) Archbishop Aldred . . . died . . . the king gave the archbishopric to one of his chaplains, Thomas . . .

35 The king gave the archbishopric of Canterbury to an elderly man called Lanfranc . . . Lanfranc, the later to be invested, was consecrated first by his own suffragans. Thomas then applied to him for consecration, but he refused unless Thomas would make profession of subjection to him. Thomas said that the rights of his church forbade him to do so, and departed without consecration,
40 reporting the actual state of the case to the king. William was annoyed at first, and sent him back to the archbishop with orders to consecrate him without insisting on the profession, but Lanfranc still refused. He came to the king, who asked him why he had not consecrated the archbishop-elect of York. He replied that the church
45 of York ought to be subject to that of Canterbury, and its elect awaiting ordination make his profession to his ordinary. Moreover, that it was expedient for the union and solidarity of the kingdom that all Britain should be subject to one primate; it might otherwise happen, in the king's time or that of one of his successors, that some
50 one of the Danes, Norwegians, or Scots, who used to sail up to York in their attacks on the realm, might be made king by the archbishop of York and the fickle and treacherous Yorkshiremen, and the kingdom disturbed and divided. Lanfranc's reputation with the Normans was such that whatever he suggested was thought certain
55 to be right.

Hugh the Chantor, *The History of the Church of York, 1066–1127*, trans. C. Johnson (London, Nelson, 1961), pp 1–3

(c) In the year of our Lord 1075, in the ninth year of the reign of William, glorious king of the English, a council of the whole land of England was assembled in the church of St. Paul the Apostle in London, namely of bishops, abbots and many ecclesiastics. The
60 council was summoned and presided over by Lanfranc, archbishop of the holy church of Canterbury and primate of the whole island of Britain . . .

Because the custom of holding councils had been in abeyance in the realm of England for many years, some legislation which is
65 already defined in ancient law was renewed.

(i) . . . the archbishop of York shall sit on the right hand of the archbishop of Canterbury, the bishop of London on his left, and Winchester next to York . . .

(ii) . . . monks shall observe a proper mode of conduct. In particular
70 the children and the young monks shall everywhere be under

supervision . . . Monks of all ages shall eschew private property . . .
(iii) . . . by the generosity of the king and the authority of the synod permission was granted to three . . . bishops . . . to move from townships to cities: Hermann from Sherborne to Salisbury, Stigand
75 from Selsey to Chichester, and Peter from Lichfield to Chester . . .
(vii) No one shall buy or sell holy orders nor any position in the Church which carries pastoral responsibility . . .
(viii) The bones of dead animals shall not be hung up anywhere as though to ward off cattle-disease; nor shall anyone cast lots, tell
80 fortunes and prophesy the future nor practise any similar works of the devil . . .
(ix) . . . no bishop or abbot nor any of the clergy shall sentence a man to be killed or mutilated; nor shall he lend the support of his authority to those who are passing sentence.

The Council of London, 1075, *The Letters of Lanfranc Archbishop of Canterbury*, eds and trans. Helen Clover and Margaret Gibson (Oxford, Clarendon Press, 1979), pp 73–9

Questions

a   Explain the following terms: (i) 'episcopal laws' (line 7); (ii) 'holy canons' (line 9); (iii) 'hundred court' (line 11); (iv) 'seat of the bishop' (line 30); (v) 'suffragans' (line 36); (vi) 'consecration' (line 37); (vii) 'ordination' (line 46); (viii) 'primate' (line 48).

b   What reason does William give in extract *a* for removing the judgement of episcopal laws from the hundred courts? Does his writ suggest that there was to be a total separation between the administration of episcopal and secular law?

c   How did Lanfranc persuade William that 'the church of York ought to be subject to that of Canterbury' (lines 44–5)?

d   In what ways, according to the evidence given in the extracts, did the English Church become a more efficient and less corrupt organisation during the reign of William I?

★   e   Why did the papacy refuse to confirm the primacy of Canterbury over York?

85 (d) I will set down here some of the new usages which William introduced to be observed throughout England. From a few examples the rest may be inferred. He would not, for instance, allow anyone in all his dominion, except on his instructions, to recognise the established Pontiff of the City of Rome as Pope or under any
90 circumstances to accept any letter from him, if it had not first been submitted to the King himself. Also he would not let the primate of his Kingdom, by which I mean the Archbishop of Canterbury . . . if he were presiding over a general council of bishops, lay down any ordinance or prohibition unless these were agreeable to the King's

95 wishes and had been first settled by him. Then again he would not
allow any one of his bishops, except on his express instructions, to
proceed against or excommunicate one of his barons or officers for
incest or adultery or any other cardinal offence, even when
notoriously guilty, or to lay upon him any punishment of
100 ecclesiastical discipline.
> *Eadmer's History of Recent Events in England: Historia Novorum
> in Anglia*, trans. G. Bosanquet (London, The Cresset Press,
> 1964), p 10

(e) At this time (1072?) the whole of Scotland with her hordes of
warriors sought to rebel against our king William and overthrow
him. He, nothing daunted, went against them with a combined force
of horse and ships . . . For he had commanded both the abbots and
105 bishops of all England to send their due knight service and he
established that from that time forward contingents of knights
should be provided by them to the kings of England in perpetual
right for their military expeditions, and that no one, however highly
placed, should presume to oppose this edict, and thus he trampled
100 underfoot the just and ancient liberties of the English Church, never
ceasing to harass it beyond endurance as though he would extinguish
it entirely.
> *Liber Eliensis* or 'The Book of Ely', trans. R. Allen Brown,
> *The Norman Conquest* (London, Edward Arnold, 1984),
> p 119

(f) King William was justly renowned for his reforming zeal; in
particular he always loved true religion in churchmen for on this the
115 peace and prosperity of the world depend. There is evidence of this
in the reputation he enjoyed everywhere, and unquestionable proof
in the works he performed. For when a bishop or abbot had come to
the end of his life and died, and God's widowed church was
mourning the loss of its head, this pious prince sent competent
120 officials to the bereaved house and had all the church property
inventoried to prevent its dilapidation by sacrilegious keepers. Then
he summoned his bishops and abbots and other prudent counsellors,
and with their advice tried to find the man most capable of governing
the house of God in both spiritual and secular matters. Finally, the
125 wise king appointed as administrator and ruler of the abbey or
bishopric whoever seemed to his highest counsellors specially
distinguished in life and doctrine. He followed this course for the
fifty-six years that he ruled the duchy of Normandy and kingdom of
England; so leaving a pious precedent for others to follow. The
130 heresy of simony was detestable to him, and so in appointing abbots
or bishops he gave less weight to wealth and power than to wisdom
and a good life. He appointed abbots of known virtue to the English
monasteries, so that by their zeal and discipline monasticism, which

for a time had been lax and faltering, revived and was restored to its
135 former strength.

> *The Ecclesiastical History of Orderic Vitalis*, ed. Marjorie
> Chibnall (6 vols, Oxford, O.U.P., 1969–80), vol II, p 239

Questions

a What was the 'heresy of simony' (line 130) and why was it 'detestable' to William?

b What evidence do the extracts provide that William 'trampled underfoot the just and ancient liberties of the English Church'?

★ c How did the composition of the prelacy change during William I's reign?

(g) Gregory, the bishop, servant of the servants of God, to his dear son in Christ, Hubert, subdeacon of the holy Roman Church, greeting and apostolic benediction . . . you have informed us that Tenzo, as legate on our behalf, has spoken against the king of
140 England. This, you should know, is not by our command. Nevertheless, the Roman Church has many things whereof to complain against him. For none of all the kings, not excepting those that are heathen, has dared to act against the apostolic see in the way he has unblushingly done; none has been so irreverent or shameless
145 as to forbid the bishops and archbishops to frequent the threshold of the apostles. Wherefore, we would have you diligently admonish him on our behalf not to strive so ardently to diminish the honour of the holy Roman Church, honour the like of which he would not release his own subjects from the obligation of according to himself;
150 so, by paying the honour due to blessed Peter, he may gain his favour.

> Letter from Pope Gregory VII to Hubert, subdeacon of the
> Roman Church, 23 September 1079, *English Historical
> Documents II 1042–1189* (2nd edn, London, 1981), p 690

(h) Gregory, the bishop, servant of the servants of God, to William, king of the English, greeting and apostolic benediction. We believe it is not hidden from your wisdom that the apostolic and royal dignities
155 excel all others in this world, and that Almighty God has apportioned his governance between them. For as he has appointed the sun and moon as lights greater than all others to show forth the beauty of the world to human eyes at diverse seasons, so, lest the creature whom his beneficence created for this world in his own
160 image should be drawn into error and mortal peril, he has provided that he should be governed by the apostolic and royal powers through their diverse offices, yet, according to the difference between the greater and the less, the Christian religion has so disposed that after God the royal power shall be governed by the care

165 and authority of the apostolic see. Although, dearest son, you are not ignorant of this, yet, in order that it may be ineradicably implanted in your mind for your salvation, Holy Scripture bears witness that the apostolic and pontifical authority must represent all kings, Christian and others, before the judgement seat of God and render an account
170 to him for their sins. If then I am to represent you in the great judgement day before the righteous Judge, the Creator of all creation, in whom is no deceit, do you prudently and carefully consider whether I should not or cannot take diligent pains for your salvation, and whether you should not or cannot without delay
175 render obedience to me, in order to possess the land of the living. Take care therefore to stand fast, to love God and place his honour before your own; serve God with a pure mind and love him with all your strength and in fullness of heart. Believe me, if you love God with a pure mind, as you now hear and as Holy Scripture
180 commands; if you place God's honour before your own in everything, he who knows no love that is counterfeit, who is powerful also to set you up, will both here and hereafter embrace you and extend to you his kingdom with his own Almighty arm.

Letter from Pope Gregory VII to William I, 8 May 1080,
English Historical Documents II 1042–1189 (2nd edn, London,
Eyre and Spottiswoode, 1981), pp 692–3

(i) To Gregory, most excellent shepherd of holy Church, William,
185 king of the English and duke of the Normans, greeting and friendship. Your legate, Hubert, most holy father, coming to me on your behalf, has admonished me to profess allegiance to you and your successors, and to think better regarding the money which my predecessors were wont to send to the Church of Rome, I have
190 consented to the one but not to the other. I have not consented to pay fealty, nor will I now, because I never promised it, nor do I find that my predecessors ever paid it to your predecessors. The money has been negligently collected during the past three years when I was in France; but now that I have returned by God's mercy to my
195 kingdom, I send you by the hands of the aforesaid legate what has already been collected, and the remainder shall be forwarded by the envoys of our trusty Archbishop Lanfranc when the opportunity for so doing shall occur. Pray for us and for the state of our realms, for we always loved your predecessors and it is our earnest desire above
200 all things to love you most sincerely, and to hear you most obediently.

Letter from William I to Pope Gregory VII, 1080, *English
Historical Documents II 1042–1189*, (2nd edn, London, Eyre
and Spottiswoode, 1981), pp 693–4

(j) The king of the English, although in certain matters he does not comport himself as devoutly as we might hope, nevertheless in that

he has neither destroyed nor sold the churches of God; that he has
205 taken pains to govern his subjects in peace and justice; that he has
refused his assent to anything detrimental to the apostolic see, even
when solicited by certain enemies of the cross of Christ; and that he
has compelled the priests on oath to put away their wives and the
laity to forward the tithes they were withholding from us – in all
210 these respects he has shown himself more worthy of approbation
and honour than other kings . . . .
   Letter from Pope Gregory VII to Hugh, bishop of Die, and
   Amatus, bishop of Oleron, 1081, *English Historical Documents
   II 1042–1189* (2nd edn, London, Eyre and Spottiswoode,
   1981), p 694

Questions

a Explain the following terms: (i) 'legate' (line 139); (ii) 'apostolic
   see' (line 143); (iii) 'tithes' (line 209).
b What is the main reason that Gregory VII wishes Hubert to
   'admonish' (line 146) William in extract *g*?
c What obligation is Gregory VII trying to impose upon William
   when he states that 'you should . . . render obedience to me, in
   order to possess the land of the living' (lines 174–5)?
d What is the significance of Gregory VII choosing 'the sun and
   moon' (line 157) to illustrate the relationship between the papacy
   and secular rulers?
e Why does William refuse to pay fealty to the pope in extract *i* and
   how does Gregory VII react to this refusal in the following
   extract?

2 The Council of Rockingham, 1095

(a) A general Council was accordingly held on that Sunday in the
church at Rockingham and from the first hour of the day the king
(William Rufus) and his followers secretly busied themselves
weaving their devices against Anselm. But Anselm called the
5 Bishops, the Abbots and the Princes to come to him from the King's
secret conclave and addressing them and a great company of monks,
clergy and laity that were in attendance said to them: "My brethren,
Sons of the Church of God, for so I call all you who are assembled
here in the name of the Lord, please pay attention and on the question
10 which you have been convened to discuss give to the best of your
ability the help of your considered opinion. Any of you who have
not yet been fully informed what that question is, please listen while
I briefly explain it. There has been some discussion between our
Lord the King and myself which seems to give rise to a specific
15 disagreement. For, when recently I asked his leave to go to Urban,

the Primate of the Apostolic See, to receive my pallium according to the custom of my predecessors, he said that he had not yet recognised this Urban as Pope and therefore he did not wish me to be in any haste to go to him for that purpose. 'Why', he said 'if in my
20 Kingdom you recognise as Pope this Urban or any one else without my choice or authority, or, having recognised him, do so hold to him, you are acting in breach of the allegiance that you owe to me and in so doing you do me no less a wrong than if you tried to take from me my crown. So you can be sure that you shall have no share
25 in my Kingdom unless I am satisfied by open avowal that you will at my wish refuse all submission of obedience to this Urban who is now in question.' I was astonished to hear him say this. I was, as you know, an Abbot in another kingdom living by the mercy of God a life free of reproach towards all men. It was not any hope or desire of
30 the archbishopric that made me come to this country but certain pressing matters which I could not possibly neglect. But at the time of the King's illness you who were then with him urgently advised him to take thought for his Mother and yours, that is, for the Church of Canterbury, and to appoint an archbishop before his death. What
35 then? Why, he took your advice and it pleased him and you to choose me for this work. I opposed it with all my might intent on escaping the primacy; but you would not have it so. Besides much else I declared openly that I had already recognised as Pope this Urban about whom this complaint is now made against me and that so long
40 as he lived I would not for a single hour depart from submission to him. At that time there was no one to say a word against me on that account. But what happened? Why, you seized hold of me and compelled me to undertake the burden of you all, me who weak and worn in body was scarce able to carry myself . . . I should that day, if
45 offered the choice, have chosen to be thrown upon a blazing pyre to be burned alive rather than to be raised to the dignity of the archbishop. But seeing the importunity of your desire I trusted myself to you and undertook the burden which you laid upon me relying upon the expectation of your help, which you then promised
50 to give me. Now then the time is come when the opportunity has presented itself for you to lighten my burden by giving me the help of your advice . . . So now, all of you, but most of all my brethren and fellow-bishops, I pray and charge you that you first look diligently into this matter and then after the most careful
55 consideration give me, as you should, advice on which I may rely, so that, while not committing any breach of the obedience I owe to the Pope, I may at the same time not offend against the allegiance which I owe to my lord the King. To me it is a terrible thing to show disrespect to and disown the Vicar of St. Peter; a terrible thing, too,
60 to transgress the allegiance which under God I have promised to maintain to the King; terrible most of all to be told that it will be

impossible for me to be true to one of these loyalties without being false to the other".

Eadmer's History of Recent Events in England: Historia Novorum in Anglia, trans. G. Bosanquet (London, The Cresset Press, 1964), pp 55-7

Questions

a For what reason does William Rufus want Anselm to 'refuse all submission of obedience' (line 26) to Urban?

b Why is Anselm 'astonished' to hear the king demand this?

c Why does Anselm regard the bishops, abbots and princes as being under an obligation to offer him advice?

★ *d* How was the dispute settled?

3 The Investiture Dispute 1100–1107

(a) Some few days after his return Anselm went to see the King (Henry I) at Salisbury. The King received him with joy and excused himself for having accepted the blessing of consecration of his royal office without waiting for the Archbishop, whose special right he
5   knew it was to give such blessing. Anselm accepted his reason and was then asked to do homage to the King in accordance with the custom of his predecessors and to receive the archbishopric from his hand. Anselm answered that he neither would nor could possibly agree to this and, when he was asked why, he at once told them quite
10 explicitly what he had heard decreed on those and certain other matters at the Council held in Rome (1099) and he went on to say this: "If my lord the King is willing to accept these decrees and accepting them to observe them, it shall be well between us and lasting peace. But, if not, I cannot see that my remaining in England
15 would be profitable or honourable; particularly as, if the King presents any bishoprics or abbeys, I must necessarily cut myself off entirely from communion, both with himself and with those who have accepted any such presentations. I have not returned to England with any intention of remaining here if the King is not willing to be
20 obedient to the Pope. So please let him declare what is his will in the matter, so that I may know what course to take." On hearing this reply of Anselm's the King was greatly perturbed. It seemed to him a terrible thing to lose the investitures of churches and homage of prelates; it seemed no less terrible to let Anselm depart from the
25 Kingdom now when he himself was not yet fully established on the throne . . . it was proposed that there should be a truce till Easter (1101) to the arguments put forward on the two sides . . .

When we had come to the Court . . . the King demanded of Anselm that he should either become his man and should consecrate,
30 as his predecessors had done before him, those to whom the King

had said that he would give bishoprics or abbeys, or alternatively should leave his country without hope of reprieve and that promptly. Anselm answered the King: "I have already told you how I was present at the Council in Rome and what I heard there from the
35 seat of St Peter. If then I, who myself introduced that sentence of excommunication in this country, for any reason render myself liable to that sentence, with whom, pray, after that can I have fellowship when I stand excommunicated by my own judgement? Envoys sent for the very purpose of having these decrees varied have
40 returned without having effected their purpose. So to tell me to make myself a transgressor of these decrees which I cannot transgress without imperilling my salvation and my honour, does not seem sound advice." The King sent this reply: "What is that to do with me? The usages of my predecessors I am not willing to lose
45 nor do tolerate anyone in my Kingdom who is not my man" . . .

On the 1st August (1107) an assembly of bishops, abbots and nobles of the realm was held in London in the King's palace. First for three successive days, without Anselm being present, the question of investitures of churches was discussed between the King and the
50 bishops, some of whom tried hard to secure that the King should continue to perform such investitures, as his father and his brother had done before him, without regard to the Pope's prohibition or the obedience due to him. The Pope, while standing fast on the sentence which had been promulgated on that matter had allowed homages,
55 which Pope Urban had prohibited equally with investitures, and had by that concession brought the King to agreement with him on the question of investitures . . . Afterwards, when Anselm was present, with the populace standing by, the King assented and declared that from that time forward no one should in England ever again be
60 invested with a bishopric or abbey by presentation of the pastoral staff or ring at the hands of the King or of any layman. Anselm on his side conceded that no one elected to any preferment in the Church should be deprived of consecration to the office to which he had been appointed because of his having done homage to the King.

Eadmer's History of Recent Events in England: Historia Novorum in Anglia, trans. G. Bosanquet (London, The Cresset Press, 1964), pp 125–6, 137–8 and 199

Questions

a Explain what is meant by the 'investitures of churches and homage of prelates' (lines 23–4).
b Why is Henry 'greatly perturbed' after his first meeting with Anselm in 1100?
c How had the nature of the argument between Henry I and Anselm changed by the time they met again in 1101?
d How is the dispute resolved in August 1107?

IV   The Social and Economic Effects of the Conquest

Introduction

Unlike the Saxon and Viking invasions and migrations, the Norman Conquest was predominantly an upper-class affair. It has been estimated that only ten thousand Normans and French settled in England before 1087 in a total population of about one and a half million, a small proportion of less than one per cent. It follows that the effects of this new order were most marked amongst the landholding and ruling classes where the old English aristocracy was almost completely displaced: there are just two recorded native landholders of significance at the end of the Conqueror's reign – Thurkill of Arden and Colswein of Lincoln.

England's new ruling class was bound together under the king by a series of obligations and tenurial arrangements confirmed by ties of homage and fealty. King William distributed the conquered territory to his supporters in return for the provision of military service. Land tenure was therefore conditional and, for a while, it established a social class permanently organised for war. The major tenants-in-chief, of whom there were about two hundred, themselves gave out fiefs to their own followers in order to meet the demands of knight service imposed by the king. Although the subject has been one of some controversy, it is now generally accepted that these processes marked the introduction of feudalism to England.

The lower reaches of society were relatively unaffected by the arrival of the Normans though the extension of royal forest land led to numerous evictions and the curtailment of grazing and other rights. Of course, the domestic military campaigns of William I's reign sometimes caused devastation, famine and depopulation, but this was not a hazard exclusive to the Norman period. Overall it seems that while the peasantry acquired foreign masters, they were not subjected to new patterns of estate management and there is little to suggest that the traditional rhythms of rural life were disrupted. Continuity was also the case with urban development except where towns, such as York, were centred in areas of resistance. Urban growth was often stimulated by programmes of castle and cathedral building, the influx of Norman tradesmen and artisans and the increased opportunities for trade with the European continent.

This chapter begins by examining William I's policy of land distribution and then proceeds to a comparison of some early feudal charters. The following section diverts attention from the top strata of society by contrasting a pre-Conquest with a twelfth-century survey of peasant services. Finally, no proper assessment of the social and economic effects of the Conquest can be made without reference to the Domesday Book regarded by F. M. Stenton as the finest administrative achievement of the medieval period. This grand survey, only conceived once the Conquest was secure, was a detailed enquiry into the condition and resources of William's new kingdom and covered all the counties in England south of the Tees and the Westmorland fells.

Further Reading

For a short but excellent introduction to the subject of English feudalism see R. Allen Brown, *The Origins of English Feudalism* (London, Allen and Unwin, 1973). Further discussion can be found in the general works already noted on p 21. An extremely readable summary of the effects of the Conquest upon English society can be found in T. Baker, *The Normans* (London, O.U.P., 1966), pp 152–68. For the Domesday survey see V. H. Galbraith, *The Making of Domesday* (Oxford, O.U.P., 1961), P. Sawyer, *Domesday Book, A Reassessment* (London, Edward Arnold, 1986) and E. M. Hallam, *Domesday Book through nine centuries* (London, Thames and Hudson, 1986).

1   The introduction of feudalism and the tenurial revolution

(a) (1066/1067) He left London and stayed for some days in a nearby place called Barking while certain fortifications were completed in the city to contain the restlessness of its vast and savage population. For he saw it was of the first importance to hold down the
5 Londoners. It was there that Edwin and Morcar, highest in degree perhaps of all the English by their birth and power, sons of the renowned Aelfgar, came in to submit to him. They besought his pardon for anything they might have done against him, and placed themselves and all their possessions in his mercy. Many other nobles
10 and magnates did the same, amongst them earl Copsi (Earl of Northumbria) . . . The king graciously accepted the oaths which they offered him, generously bestowed his favour upon them, restored to them all their possessions, and held them in great honour.
    Proceeding thence, he came to divers parts of the kingdom,
15 arranging everything to his convenience and that of the inhabitants. Wherever he went all laid down their arms. There was no resistance, but everywhere men submitted to him or sought his peace . . . The aetheling (Edgar) himself, whom after the fall of Harold the English

had thought to make king, he endowed with wide lands and took
20 into the closest circle of his affection because he was of the race of
king Edward, and also so that the boy in his youth should not too
bitterly regret the loss of the honour to which he had once been
chosen. Many English received by his liberal gift more than they had
ever received from their fathers or their former lords. He placed
25 capable castellans with ample forces of horse and foot in his castles,
men brought over from France in whose loyalty no less than
competence he could trust. He gave them rich fiefs in return for
which they willingly endured hardship and danger. But to no
Frenchman was anything given unjustly taken from an Englishman.

> William of Poitiers, *Gesta Willelmi ducis Normannorum et regis
> Anglorum*, trans. R. Allen Brown, *The Norman Conquest*
> (London, Edward Arnold, 1984), pp 38–9

30 (b) After King William had defeated the leading Mercian earls as I
have related – Edwin being dead and Morcar languishing in prison –
he divided up the chief provinces of England amongst his followers,
and made the humblest of the Normans men of wealth, with civil
and military authority . . .
35   King William gave the county of Northampton to Earl Waltheof,
son of Siward, one of the greatest of the English, and married him to
his own niece Judith to strengthen the bonds of friendship between
them; later she bore her husband two beautiful daughters.
    Likewise Eustace count of Boulogne, Robert of Mortain, William
40 of Evreux, and Robert of Eu and Geoffrey son of Rotrou of
Mortagne and other earls and magnates too numerous to name
received great revenues and fiefs in England from King William. So
foreigners grew wealthy with the spoils of England, whilst her own
sons were either shamefully slain or driven as exiles to wander
45 hopelessly through foreign kingdoms. It is said that the king himself
received each day in sterling money a thousand and sixty-one
pounds ten shillings and three halfpence from the ordinary revenue
of England, not counting royal tribute and judicial fines and many
other sources of revenue which daily swelled the royal treasure . . .
50 he allocated land to knights and arranged their contingents in such a
way that the kingdom of England should always have 60,000
knights, ready to be mustered at a moment's notice in the king's
service whenever necessary.

> *The Ecclesiastical History of Orderic Vitalis*, ed. Marjorie
> Chibnall (Oxford, O.U.P., 1969), vol II, pp 261–7

Questions

a Explain the following terms: (i) 'castellans' (line 25); (ii) 'fiefs'
(line 27); (iii) 'knights' (line 50).
b What evidence is there in the extracts that King William

originally intended to form an Anglo-Norman state with a mixed pattern of landholding? Is this evidence open to other interpretation?

c   What does Orderic Vitalis tell us about the distribution of lands in 1071 to which year extract *b* refers?

(c) In the year of the Incarnation of our Lord, one thousand and
55 eighty-three. We Gilbert, the abbot, and the convent of Westminster have given to William Baynard a certain farm in the township of Westminster, by name 'Totenhala' to house him, and to be held by him for the whole of his life by the service of 1 knight. This is to be held by him with all things that pertain to it, as well and freely as ever
60 Wulfric the thegn surnamed 'Bordewayte' held it from the church. Therefore William shall himself have the customs and the liberties which we have in the same, always excepting the aids which we shall receive from our knights, as is done on the other lands of the church, and always excepting the tithes of this land which are assigned to our
65 house in alms. We have granted these things to be held by him because of the love and service he has shown to our church; but on the condition that after his death the aforesaid land may remain bound to our church and quit of obligations. And in respect of this, the aforesaid William has pledged us that he will neither sell this land
70 nor place it in pawn nor alienate it to anyone to the loss of our church. Witness: Robert the prior; William and Herbert, monks; Ralph Bainard; Herlvin, brother of Gunzo; and many others.
      Charter of abbot Gilbert and the convent of Westminster to William Baynard, 1083, *English Historical Documents II 1042–1189* (2nd edn, London, Eyre and Spottiswoode, 1981), pp 960–1

(d) Be it known to all of you that Peter, a knight of King William, will become the feudal man of St. Edmund and of Baldwin the
75 abbot, by performing the ceremony of homage. He will do this by permission of the king and with the consent of the monks, and in return for the service which will here be stated, saving always the fealty which he owes to the king, the fief having been truly received except for the six royal forfeitures. Peter promises that he will serve
80 on behalf of the abbot within the kingdom with 3 or 4 knights at their own expense if he has been previously summoned by the king and the abbot to take part in the earlier or later levies of the king's host. If he is bidden to plead on the abbot's behalf at any place within the kingdom, they shall likewise bear their own expense. But if the
85 abbot shall take him anywhere else, then the expense of his service shall be borne by the abbot. Besides this, he shall equip a knight for service without or within the kingdom where and when the abbot shall require to have this knight as his own retainer . . . Witnesses

on behalf of the abbot: Robert Blunt; Frodo . . . Jocelyn. Witnesses
90   on behalf of Peter: Rannulf; Richard; Herdwin. . . .
Charter of Baldwin, abbot of Bury St. Edmunds in favour of
Peter, a knight of King William, 1066–1087, *English
Historical Documents II 1042–1189* (2nd edn, London, Eyre
and Spottiswoode, 1981), p 961

(e) This privilege Robert, bishop of the church of Hereford, ordered
to be recorded as agreed between him and Roger, son of Walter
concerning certain land which is called 'Hamme', and those things
which pertain to it. This land belongs to the church of Holy Mary,
95   the Mother of God, and of St. Ethelbert the martyr; and previously
the said bishop held this land as his own demesne and for the
sustenance of the church. This land the aforesaid knight, to wit,
Roger, asked from the bishop through friends, and he offered
money in respect of it. But the bishop, by the counsel of his vassals,
100   gave him this same land in return for a promise that he would serve
the bishop with 2 knights as his father did whenever the need arose.
This also was part of the contract: that the men of the bishop
belonging to the King's Hampton and Hereford, and to the estates
pertaining thereto, should be at liberty to take timber from the wood
105   for the use of the bishop as often as it should be needed for fuel or for
repairing houses; and the pigs of these manors should feed in the
same wood. This refers to the men belonging to the bishop. And this
contract further enjoins that if Roger becomes a monk, or dies,
neither his mother nor his wife nor his sons nor his brothers nor any
110   of his kinsfolk shall have rights in the aforesaid land, but let the
bishop receive whatever in the estate may be to the profit of holy
Church, and his men shall receive the same without any
contradiction whatsoever. This instrument was executed in the year
of the Incarnation of our Lord 1085, it being the eighth Indiction.
115   The following were witnesses to this matter: Earl Roger, and his
son, Hugh, and his other son, Everard, and the Countess . . . Of the
men of the bishop there were there: Gerald, his brother; Humphrey,
the archdeacon . . .
Charter of Robert bishop of Hereford to Roger son of Walter,
1085, *English Historical Documents II 1042–1189* (2nd edn,
London, Eyre and Spottiswoode, 1981), p 962

Questions

a   Explain the following terms: (i) 'aids' (line 62); (ii) 'ceremony of
homage' (line 75); (iii) 'fealty' (line 78); (iv) 'demesne' (line 96).
b   What restrictions or obligations does William Baynard have to
accept in return for 'Totenhala' (line 57)?
c   How does Baldwin benefit from Peter becoming his 'feudal man'
(line 74)?

d How is the relationship between Peter and Baldwin affected by royal power?

e What does extract *e* disclose about the history of 'Hamme' up to the date of the charter?

f What rights were granted to the bishop's men of King's Hampton and Hereford by Robert of Hereford's charter?

2 The condition of the peasantry

(a) *Thegn's Law*. The law of the thegn is that he be entitled to his book-right, and he shall contribute three things in respect of his land: armed service, and the repairing of fortresses and work on bridges. Also in respect of many estates, further service arises on the king's
5 order such as service connected with the deer fence at the king's residence, and equipping a guard ship, and guarding the coast, and guarding the lord, and military watch, almsgiving and church dues and many other various things.

Geneat's Right. Geneat-right is various according to what is fixed in
10 respect of the estate: in some he must pay rent and contribute a pasturage swine a year, ride and perform carrying service and furnish means of carriage, work and entertain his lord, reap and mow, cut deer hedges and keep up places from which deer may be shot, build and fence the lord's house, bring strangers to the village,
15 pay church dues and alms money, act as guard to his lord, take care of the horses, and carry messages far and near wheresoever he is directed.

Cottar's-Right. The cottar's right is according to the custom of the estate: in some he must work for his lord each Monday throughout
20 the year, or 3 days each week at harvest-time . . . He does not make land payment. He should have 5 acres: more if it be the custom on the estate; and it is too little if it ever be less; because his work must be frequent. Let him give his hearth-penny on Ascension Day even as each freeman ought to do. Let him also perform services on his lord's
25 demesne-land if he is ordered, by keeping watch on the sea-coast and working at the king's deer fence and such things according to his condition. Let him pay his church dues at Martinmas.

Boor's Right. The boor's duties are various, in some places heavy and in others light. On some estates the custom is that he must perform
30 week-work for 2 days in each week of the year as he is directed, and 3 days from the Feast of the Purification to Easter. If he perform carrying service he need not work while his horse is out. At Michaelmas he must pay 10 pence for gafol (rent or tribute), and at Martinmas 23 sesters of barley, and 2 hens, and at Easter a young
35 sheep or 2 pence. And he must lie from Martinmas to Easter at his lord's fold as often as it falls to his lot; and from the time when ploughing is first done until Martinmas he must each week plough 1 acre, and himself present the seed in the lord's barn. Also (he must

plough) 3 acres as boonwork, and 2 for pasturage. If he needs more
40 grass, let him earn it as he may be permitted. Let him plough 3 acres
as his tribute land and sow it from his own barn, and pay his
hearth-penny. And every pair of boors must maintain 1 hunting
dog, and each boor must give 6 loaves to the herdsman of the lord's
swine when he drives his herd to the mast-pasture. On the same land
45 to which the customs apply a farmer ought to be given for his
occupation of the land 2 oxen, 1 cow, 6 sheep and 7 acres sown on his
rood of land. After that year let him perform all the dues that fall to
him, and let him be given tools for his work and utensils for his
house. When death befalls him let the lord take charge of what he
50 leaves.

The estate-law is fixed on each estate: at some places, as I have
said, it is heavier, at some places, also, lighter, because not all
customs about estates are alike. On some estates a boor must pay
tribute in honey, on some in food, on some in ale. Let him who has
55 the shire always know what are the ancient arrangements about the
estate and what is the custom of the district . . .

A swine-herd at pay ought to pay for his animals that are to be
slaughtered according to the amount fixed on the estate. On many
estates it is fixed that he pay every year 15 swine for killing, 10 old
60 and 5 young. Let him have himself whatever he raises beyond that.
On many estates a more severe due is incumbent on the swine-herd.
Let each swine-herd take care that after the slaughter of his swine he
prepare them properly and singe them: then he will be well entitled
to the perquisites. Also he must be . . . always ready for every sort of
65 work, and provided with a horse at the lord's need.

Rectitudines Singularum Personarum or 'The Rights and Ranks
of People', first half of the eleventh century, *English Historical
Documents II 1042–1189*, (2nd edn, London, Eyre and
Spottiswoode, 1981), pp 875–7

(b) This is the description of the manors of the abbey of
Peterborough as Walter the archdeacon received them and possessed
them in the hand of the king.

In Kettering are 10 hides for the king's geld. And of these 10 hides
70 40 villeins hold 40 virgates. And these men plough in the spring from
each virgate 4 acres for the work of the lord. And besides this they
provide ploughs for the work of the lord four times in the winter,
and three times in the spring and once in the summer. And these men
have 22 ploughs with which they work. And all these men work for
75 the lord 3 days in each week. And besides this they render each year
from each virgate by custom 2 shillings and 3 half pence. And shall
the men render 50 hens and 640 eggs. And besides this, Ailric holds
13 acres with 2 acres of meadow, and pays for them 16 pence. And
there is a mill with a miller and it pays 20 shillings. And 8 cottars each

80 of whom has 5 acres and they work (for the lord) 1 day each week, and twice a year they make malt. And each one of them gives 1 penny for a he-goat (if he has one) and 1 halfpenny for a nanny-goat. And there is a shepherd and a swine-herd who holds 8 acres. And in the court of the demesne there are 4 ploughs with 32 oxen, and 12

85 cows with 10 calves, 2 beasts for food, 3 draught horses, 300 sheep, 50 pigs, and 16 shillings' worth of the surplus hay from the meadow. The church of Kettering belongs to the altar of the abbey of Peterborough. And for the love of St. Peter it renders 4 rams and 2 cows or 5 shillings . . .

90   In Thorpe Achurch are 2 hides and 1 virgate for the king's geld. And there are 12 full villeins and each one of them holds 11 acres and works (for the lord) 3 days each week. And 6 half-villeins who perform the same in proportion to their holdings. And all of these make a customary payment of 10 shillings. And besides this they pay

95 for love of St. Peter 5 'multones', and 10 ells of cloth, and 10 baskets and 200 loaves. And all these men plough 16½ acres for the lord's work. And there are 6 borders who pay 7 shillings. And all these pay each year 22 skepfuls of oats in return for dead wood and 22 loaves and 64 hens and 160 eggs. And one sokeman is there who performs

100 service with a horse. And William, son of Ansered, holds a fourth part of 3 yard lands by service in the abbot's kitchen. And the men of this William perform work for the court, that is to say, they provide their ploughs for the lord twice a year. And on the land of this William there are 4 full villeins who reap half an acre in August. And

105 Godric holds a fourth part of 3 yard lands, and for that he and his horse do the abbot's service, providing their own food. And this Godric has 3 villeins and each one of them reaps half an acre for the abbot in August, and with their ploughs they perform two boon-works. In the court of the demesne there are 2 ploughs with 16

110 oxen, and 3 cows and 8 beasts for food and 1 draught horse and 8 pigs.

     In Collingham there are 4 carucates and 1 bovate less a fifth part of 1 bovate for the king's geld. And there are 20 villeins who hold 1½ carucates. Each one of these works for the lord throughout the year 1

115 day each week. And in August he performs 3 boon-works. And all these men bring 60 cartloads of wood to the lord's court, and they also dig and provide 20 cartloads of turves, or 20 cartloads of thatch. And they must harrow throughout the winter. And each year they pay 4 pounds of rent. And there are 50 sokemen who hold 2½

120 carucates of land. And each one of these must work by custom each year for 6 days at the deer hedge. And in August each shall work 3 days. And all these have 14 ploughs and with them they shall work for the lord four times in Lent. And they plough 48 acres, and harrow, and reap in August. And the aforesaid sokemen pay 12

125 pounds each year. And in the court of the demesne are 2 ploughs

with 16 oxen, and 4 cows and calves and 1 beast for food and 160 sheep and 12 pigs . . .

A survey of three manors belonging to the abbey of Peterborough taken from the Black Book of Peterborough, 1125–1128, *English Historical Documents II* (2nd edn, London, Eyre and Spottiswoode, 1981), pp 892–3

Questions

a   Explain the following terms: (i) 'week-work' (line 30); (ii) 'kings geld' (line 69); (iii) 'boon-works' (line 109); (iv) 'carucate' (line 112); (v) 'bovate' (line 112).

b   What evidence is there in the first extract for the existence of local variation in the pattern of labour obligation?

c   How do the obligations of the villeins of Kettering (lines 69–77) compare with those of Collingham (lines 112–19)?

d   In what sense do the contents of the two extracts suggest that they were written for different purposes?

e   Do comparisons between the villeins' obligations in the Peterborough surveys and those of the boor in the *Rectitudines* . . . , enable us to draw any conclusions regarding the changing status of the peasantry during the Norman Conquest?

3   The Domesday Survey

(a) 1085. In this year men reported and declared it to be true that Cnut, king of Denmark, son of king Swein, was on his way hither, determined to conquer this country with the help of count Robert of Flanders, since Cnut had married Robert's daughter. When king
5   William learnt of this – he was then residing in Normandy because he owned both England and Normandy – he returned to England with a vast host of horse and foot from France and Brittany which was greater than any that had ever come to this country. It was so vast that men wondered how this land could feed such a host. The king,
10   however, had the host spread over the whole country, quartering them with each of his vassals according to the produce of his estate. Men suffered great hardship during the same year, for the king gave orders for the coastal districts to be laid waste, so that if his enemies landed they would find nothing which could be quickly seized . . .
15   The king spent Christmas with his councillors at Gloucester, and held his court there for five days . . .

After this the king had important deliberations and exhaustive discussions with his council about this land, how it was peopled, and with what sort of men. Then he sent his men all over England into
20   every shire to ascertain how many hundreds of 'hides' of land there were in each shire, and how much land and live-stock the king himself owned in the country, and what annual dues were lawfully his from each shire. He also had it recorded how much land his

archbishops had, and his diocesan bishops, his abbots and his earls,
25 and – though I may be going into too great detail – and what or how
much each man who was a landholder here in England had in land or
in live-stock, and how much money it was worth. So very
thoroughly did he have the inquiry carried out that there was not a
single 'hide', not one virgate of land, not even – it is shameful to
30 record it, but it did not seem shameful to him to do – not even one
ox, nor one cow, nor one pig which escaped notice in his survey.
And all the surveys were subsequently brought to him . . . (1086).
In this year the king . . . dubbed his son Henry knight. Thereafter
he journeyed around the country so that he came to Salisbury by
35 Lammas, where he was met by his council and all the landholders
who were of any account throughout England, no matter whose
vassals they might be. All did him homage and became his men, and
swore him oaths of allegiance that they would be faithful to him
against all other men . . . he purposed to go to Normandy . . . First,
40 however, he did as he was wont, he levied very heavy taxes on his
subjects, upon any pretext, whether justly or unjustly . . .

> Peterborough version (E) of *The Anglo-Saxon Chronicle*,
> trans. G. N. Garmonsway (London, Dent, 1953), pp 215–17

(b) In the twentieth year of his reign by order of William, king of the
English, there was made a survey of the whole of England, that is to
say, of the lands of the several provinces of England, and of the
45 possessions of each and all of the magnates. This was done in respect
of plough land and habitations, and of men both bond and free, both
those who dwelt in cottages, and those who had their homes and
their share in the fields; and in respect of ploughs and horses and
other animals; and in respect of the services and payments due from
50 all men in the whole land. Other investigators followed the first, and
men were sent into provinces which they did not know, and where
they were themselves unknown, in order that they might be given
the opportunity of checking the first survey and, if necessary, of
denouncing its authors as guilty to the king. And the land was vexed
55 with much violence arising from the collection of the royal taxes.

> Note added by Robert Losinga, bishop of Hereford, 1079–
> 1095, to the chronicle of Marianus Scotus, *English Historical
> Documents II 1042–1189*, (2nd edn, London, Eyre and
> Spottiswoode, 1981), p 912

(c) . . . the inquiry concerning lands which the king's barons made
according to the oath of the sheriff of the shire and of all the barons
and their Frenchmen, and of the whole hundred court – the priest,
reeve and 6 villeins from each village. They inquired what the manor
60 was called; who held it in the time of King Edward; who holds it
now; how many hides there are; how many ploughs in demesne and
how many belonging to the men; how many villeins; how many
cottars; how many slaves; how many freemen; how many sokemen;

how much woodland; how much meadow; how much pasture; how
65 many mills; how many fisheries; how much has been added to, or
taken away from, the estate; what it used to be worth altogether;
what it is worth now; and how much each freeman and sokeman had
and has. All this to be recorded thrice: to wit, as it was in the time of
King Edward, as it was when King William gave the estate, and as it
70 is now. And it was also noted whether more could be taken from the
estate than is now being taken.

> Prologue to The Ely Inquest, c. 1086, *English Historical*
> *Documents II 1042–1189* (2nd edn, London, Eyre and
> Spottiswoode, 1981), p 946

Questions

a Is there any connection between the threatened Danish invasion
(lines 1–14) and William's decision to instigate the Domesday
survey?

b What measures, according to extracts *b* and *c*, did William take to
ensure the accuracy of the information recorded in Domesday?

c Explain the following terms: (i) 'reeve' (line 59); (ii) 'freemen'
(line 63); (iii) 'sokemen' (line 63); (iv) 'cottars' (line 63).

d For what purpose could William have required the Domesday
information to be recorded three times: 'as it was in the time of
King Edward, as it was when King William gave the estate, and
as it is now' (lines 68–70)? What factors might have caused the
value of an estate to fall between 1066 and 1087?

e What do the extracts reveal about William's motives for
authorising the Domesday survey?

(d) Hundred of Dunmow. Asgar held (High) Easter before 1066 as a
manor, for 2 hides. Now Geoffrey holds it in lordship. Always 4
ploughs in lordship; 12 men's ploughs. Then 46 villagers, now 47;
75 then 14 smallholders, now 33; always 9 slaves. Woodland, 600 pigs;
Meadow, 30 acres; 5 ploughs possible in lordship. Then 3 cobs, 7
cattle, 60 pigs, 60 sheep, 30 goats, 10 beehives; now 3 cobs, 7 cows,
27 pigs, 50 sheep, 4 goats, 17 beehives. Value then and later £20; now
(£)30.

80 Attached to this manor have always been 6 Freemen with 1½
hides. Then 2 ploughs, now 1. Now 3 smallholders. Meadow, 8
acres. Value then 20s; now 30(s).

Also attached to this manor, 2 hides and 1 virgate which 2
Freemen held before 1066. On them have always been 4 ploughs in
85 lordship and 1½ men's ploughs. Then 8 villagers, now 7; then 6
smallholders, now 7; always 3 slaves. Woodland, 60 pigs; meadow,
24 acres. Value then and later 100s; now £10. 3 men-at-arms hold this
from Geoffrey.

Also attached to this manor is ½ hide which belonged to the

90 church of the manor before 1066. Now Gutbert holds it from
Geoffrey. Always 1 plough. Then 1 smallholder, now 3; 1 slave.
Woodland, 20 pigs, meadow, 5 acres. Value then 20s; now 30(s).
   The Abbot of Ely lays claim to the above-mentioned manor and
the Hundred testifies that it was in (the lands of) the Abbey before
95 1066; but Asgar held this manor in 1066.
   Domesday Survey of the manor of High Easter, *Domesday
   Book*, gen. ed. John Morris, vol 32, Essex, ed. Alexander
   Rumble, trans. Judy Plaister and Veronika Sankaran
   (Chichester, Philimore, 1983), p 606

Questions

a Explain the following terms: (i) 'hundred' (line 72); (ii) 'virgate'
    (line 83); (iii) 'hide' (line 89).
b Explain the meaning of '4 ploughs in lordship' (lines 73–4).
c Comment on the fact that the value of High Easter has risen from
    £20 to £30 (lines 78–9).
d How far does the information provided on the manor of High
    Easter conform to the lines of enquiry set down in extract *c*?

V The Death of William Rufus

Introduction

William Rufus was killed by an arrow while hunting in the New Forest in the late afternoon of Thursday, 2 August 1100. It is commonly assumed that he was shot by his friend Walter Tirel. By the evening of the same day William's younger brother, Henry, had gone to Winchester and taken possession of the royal treasure. On the next day Rufus was buried at Winchester and Henry was elected king by a hastily-assembled council. On Sunday, 5 August Henry was crowned in Westminster Abbey by Maurice, bishop of London. Both archbishops were absent, and Henry's eldest brother, Robert, duke of Normandy, had not yet arrived back in Normandy after the First Crusade.

William Rufus' death has excited the imaginations of several historians. By combining uncritically contemporary and later sources together with anthropological evidence of witchcraft rites, Margaret Murray, an anthopologist herself, argued in *God of Witches* that Rufus was the victim of a ritual killing in a pagan fertility cult. This view has received some support, but is not accepted by professional historians.

Henry's swift actions after his brother's death have aroused the suspicions of some. Murder by Henry, or at least murder arranged with Henry's complicity, is one possible explanation of Rufus' sudden death. Other circumstances surrounding his death have enabled some historians to develop their views that Henry was involved in Rufus' murder still further. According to many contemporary accounts, Rufus' death was preceded by supernatural events. Springs bubbled with blood. Monks had terrifying dreams foretelling Rufus' death. These supernatural events have been interpreted occasionally as evidence that there was a plot to remove Rufus from the throne, and that the existence of this plot had been quite widely known amongst the upper echelons of English society. Murder is seen, too, because Henry is said to have rewarded certain nobles excessively in the course of his reign. The Clare and Gifford families attained particular favour. Such favour was especially damning evidence because the Clares and the Giffords were related by marriage to Walter Tirel. Finally, in the eyes of the murder-plot historians, Henry had a pressing motive to seize the throne in the summer of 1100. His eldest brother, Robert, duke of Normandy was returning to Normandy. He had pawned the duchy to William Rufus in 1096 to raise the money to go on the First Crusade. In 1100 Robert was on his way home, with a beautiful young wife in tow, who would, no doubt, bear him children. If Henry did not act before his arrival, his chances of attaining control of either England or Normandy would disappear completely.

However, the conspiracy theory of Rufus' death has been called into question. Doubts have been cast upon it by two parallel lines of argument. The first examines the contemporary or near contemporary evidence in great detail and very critically to reveal flaws in several elements of the murder-plot story. For example, it is apparent that we cannot be sure of the identity of Rufus' companions on the day of his death. Some doubt exists whether Walter Tirel actually fired the arrow which killed Rufus. Secondly by looking at the circumstances of Rufus' death in a wider perspective the existence of a plot becomes much less conclusive. C. Warren Hollister remarks that it was not unusual for a successor to act quickly to secure his predecessor's throne: 'At Henry I's own death in 1135, Stephen of Blois dashed from Boulogne to London, was elected king, rushed to Winchester for the treasure, then back to Westminster for the coronation'. William Rufus had even left Rouen to take the English crown before his father died. Accidental deaths while hunting were not uncommon. Richard, the son of William the Conqueror, had been fatally injured in the New Forest by colliding with a tree while chasing a stag. In 1100 Robert Curthose's bastard son Richard had been shot accidentally while hunting in the same forest. Fantastic tales presaging violent death were not so much indications of the existence of a conspiracy as the necessary explanations in the writings of religious men of the death of a king who was widely held to have offended God. Detailed research shows that the Clares and the Giffords were not shown particular favour by Henry I. They were great and powerful men who would have received reward whoever was king. Finally, the imminent return of Robert Curthose, duke of Normandy, did not represent Henry's last chance of attaining real power. There was no guarantee that Rufus was going to relinquish Normandy readily. Nor was there any certainty that Rufus would automatically have been succeeded by Robert or Robert's children in the event of Rufus' death if Robert had been reinstated in Normandy.

Further Reading

The best review of the circumstances surrounding Rufus' death is C. Warren Hollister, 'The Strange Death of William Rufus', *Speculum*, vol XLVIII (1973), pp 637–53. Hollister's line is largely followed by F. Barlow, *William Rufus* (London, Methuen, 1983).

This is now the essential starting point for serious work on the reign of William Rufus. As brief introductions the relevant chapters in C. Brook, *The Saxon & Norman Kings* (Glasgow, Fontana, 1967) and F. Barlow, *The Feudal Kingdom of England, 1042–1216* (3rd edn, London, Longman, 1972) are to be recommended.

1 The Anglo-Saxon Chronicle's account of Rufus' death

(a) On Whit Sunday of this year (1100) at a village in Berkshire, blood was seen bubbling forth from the ground, as many reported who were said to have seen it. And thereafter, on the morning after Lammas (1 August) king William was killed with an arrow while
5 hunting by one of his men. He was afterwards brought to Winchester and buried in the Cathedral.

> *The Anglo-Saxon Chronicle*, trans. G. N. Garmonsway, (Everyman edn, London, Dent, 1953), p 235

Question

Why is extract *a* significant?

2 William of Malmesbury's account of William Rufus' death

(b) The day before the king died, he dreamed that he was let blood by a surgeon; and that the stream, reaching to heaven, clouded the light, and intercepted the day. Calling on St. Mary for protection, he suddenly awoke, commanded a light to be brought, and forbade his
5 attendants to leave him. They then watched with him several hours until daylight. Shortly after, just as the day began to dawn, a certain foreign monk told Robert Fitz Hamon, one of the principal nobility, that he had that night dreamed a strange and fearful dream about the king: "That he had come into a certain church, with menacing and
10 insolent gestures, as was his custom, looking contemptuously on the standers by; then violently seizing the crucifix, he gnawed the arms, and almost tore away the legs: that the image endured this for a long time, but at length struck the king with its foot in such a manner that he fell backwards: from his mouth, as he lay prostrate, issued so
15 copious a flame that the volumes of smoke touched the very stars." Robert, thinking that this dream ought not to be neglected, as he was intimate with him, immediately related it to the king. William, repeatedly laughing, exclaimed, "He is a monk, and dreams for money like a monk; give him a hundred shillings." Nevertheless,
20 being greatly moved, he hesitated a long while whether he should go out to hunt, as he had designed: his friends persuading him not to suffer the truth of the dreams to be tried at his personal risk. In

consequence, he abstained from the chase before dinner, dispelling
the uneasiness of his unregulated mind by serious business.
25   They relate, that, having plentifully regaled that day, he soothed his
cares with a more than usual quantity of wine. After dinner he went
into the forest, attended by a few persons; of whom the most intimate with him was Walter, surnamed Tirel, who had been induced to
come from France by the liberality of the king. This man alone had
30   remained with him, while the others, employed in the chase, were
dispersed as chance directed. The sun was now declining, when the
king, drawing his bow and letting fly an arrow, slightly wounded a
stag which passed before him; and, keenly gazing, followed it, still
running, a long time with his eyes, holding up his hand to keep off
35   the power of the sun's rays. At this instant Walter, conceiving a
noble exploit, which was while the king's attention was otherwise
occupied to transfix another stag which by chance came near him,
unknowingly, and without power to prevent it, Oh, gracious God!
pierced his breast with a fatal arrow. On receiving the wound, the
40   king uttered not a word; but breaking off the shaft of the weapon
where it projected from his body, fell upon the wound, by which he
accelerated his death. Walter immediately ran up, but as he found
him senseless and speechless, he leaped swiftly upon his horse, and
escaped by spurring him to his utmost speed. Indeed there was none
45   to pursue him: some connived at his flight; others pitied him; and all
were intent on other matters. Some began to fortify their dwellings;
others to plunder; and the rest to look out for a new king. A few
countrymen conveyed the body, placed on a cart, to the cathedral at
Winchester; the blood dripping from it all the way. There it was
50   committed to the ground within the tower, attended by many of the
nobility, though lamented by few. Next year, the tower fell; though
I forbear to mention the different opinions on this subject lest I
should seem to assent too readily to unsupported trifles, more
especially as the building might have fallen through imperfect
55   construction, even though he had never been buried there.

William of Malmesbury's Chronicle of the Kings of England, ed.
J. A. Giles (London, Henry G. Bohn, 1847), pp 344–6

Questions

a   Why does William of Malmesbury concentrate so much on
     Rufus' dream and the monk's dream?
b   What features of extract b could be used to support the view that
     there was a plot to kill William Rufus?
c   Explain why 'all were intent on other matters' (lines 45–6)
     immediately after Rufus' death.
d   Explain William of Malmesbury's views about the collapse of the
     tower at Winchester Cathedral.

3 Orderic Vitalis and the death of William Rufus

(c) The next morning King William sat at meat with his intimates, making preparation to go hunting in the New Forest after dinner. As he was laughing and joking with his attendants and pulling on his boots, a smith arrived and offered him six arrows.

5 He took them eagerly, praised the maker for his work and, ignorant of what was in store, kept four for himself and handed two to Walter Tirel . . . one of the king's close friends and his constant companion everywhere.

. . . (Then) he sprang to his feet and, mounting his horse, galloped
10 into the wood. His brother Count Henry, William of Breteuil, and other eminent men were there; they entered the wood and sent the huntsmen off into different places as was customary. The king and Walter (Tirel) of Poix were stationed in the wood with a few companions; as they stood on the alert waiting for their prey with
15 their weapons ready a beast suddenly ran between them. The king drew back from his place, and Walter let fly an arrow. It sped swiftly over the beast's back, grazing the hair, and mortally wounded the king who was standing directly in its path. He fell to the ground, and, dreadful to relate, died at once. When this one mortal perished
20 many were thrown into great confusion, and terrible shouts that the king was dead rang through the wood. Henry galloped at top speed to Winchester castle where the royal treasure was, and imperiously demanded the keys from the keepers as the lawful heir . . . The moment the king was dead many nobles made off from the wood to
25 their estates, and prepared to resist the disorders they anticipated. Some of the humbler attendants covered the king's bloody body as best they might with wretched clothes and carried him like a wild boar stuck with spears from the wood to the town of Winchester. The clergy and the monks and poorer citizens only, with widows
30 and beggars came out to meet him and, out of reverence for the royal dignity, quickly buried him in the old minster of St. Peter. But the doctors and prelates of the Church, considering his squalid life and dreadful death, ventured to pass judgment, declaring that he was virtually past redemption and unworthy of absolution by the
35 Church, since as long as he lived they had never been able to turn him from his vices to salvation. In some churches bells that had often sounded long peals for the meanest of the poor and for common women were not rung for him. From the huge treasure-store, where many heaps of coins wrung from the labours of the poor were piled
40 up, no alms were given to the needy for the soul of the miser who had once possessed it. However, mercenary soldiers, lechers, and common harlots lost their wages through the death of the lascivious king, and lamented his wretched end not through respect but out of vile greed that fed on his vices; these sought desperately for Walter
45 Tirel to rend him limb from limb for the death of their protector. But

the moment the deed was done he hurried to the coast, crossed the sea, and made for his castles in France, where he laughed in safety at the threats and curses of those who wished to harm him.

> *The Ecclesiastical History of Orderic Vitalis*, ed. Marjorie Chibnall (6 vols, Oxford, O.U.P., 1969–80), vol V, pp 289–93

Questions

a What evidence is contained in extract *c* for the view that the king was irreligious?

b What evidence is contained in extract *c* for the view that the king's death was an accident?

c What new elements do extracts *b* and *c* introduce to extract *a*'s account of William's death?

d In what ways do extracts *b* and *c* differ in their accounts of the king's attitude and actions before the hunt?

* e Explain the reference to 'mercenary soldiers, lechers and common harlots' (lines 41–2) in William Rufus' reign.

4 Eadmer and the death of William Rufus

(d) On that day after having breakfasted he went out into the forest to hunt and there, struck by an arrow that pierced his heart, impenitent and unconfessed, he died instantly and was at once forsaken by everyone. Whether, as some say, that arrow struck him in its flight,
5 or, as the majority declare, he stumbled and falling violently upon it met his death, is a question we think it unnecessary to go into; sufficient to know that by the just judgment of God he was stricken down and slain . . . This news (of the king's death) came as a great shock to Anselm and he was presently so overcome that he wept
10 most bitterly. We were greatly surprised to see him so affected; but he, his voice broken with sobs, declared in very truth, from which no servant of God can rightly stray, that, had it been possible to choose, he would much rather that he himself had suffered this death of the body than that the king, as he was, should do so.

> *Eadmer's History of Recent Events in England: Historia Novorum in Anglia*, trans. G. Bosanquet (London, The Cresset Press, 1964), pp 120–3

Questions

* a Explain the background to the bad relations between William Rufus and Anselm.

b What do extracts *b*, *c* and *d* have in common in their explanations of the underlying causes of Rufus' death?

5 Tirel's role

(e) Some people alleged that a certain nobleman, Walter Tirel, had shot the king with an arrow. But we often heard him claim on oath, at a time when he had nothing to fear nor to hope for, that on that day he had neither come into that part of the forest where the king had
5 been hunting, nor seen him at all in the forest.

Suger, *Vie de Louis VI le Gros*, ed. et trad. H. Waquet (Paris, Société d'Edition, 'Les Belles Lettres', 1964), pp 12–13

Questions

a What is the significance of Suger's words 'at a time when he had nothing to fear nor to hope for' (line 3)?

b Compare extracts *b*, *c*, *d* and *e*. What conclusions do these extracts allow us to draw about Tirel's role in the death of William Rufus?

6 A more favourable view of William Rufus

(f) In the forest was the king,
In the thicket, near a marsh.
He wanted to shoot at a stag
Which he saw pass in a herd.
5 Near a tree he dismounted.
He bent his bow himself.
On all sides the barons dismounted.
The others surrounded the place.
Walter Tirel dismounted
10 Very near the king, close to an elder,
Against an aspen he leaned.
As the herd passed,
And the great hart came in the midst,
He drew the bow which he held in his hand,
15 A barbed arrow
He shot, by an evil fate.
Now it befel that he missed the hart,
And to the heart he struck the king.
An arrow went to his heart.
20 But we know not who drew the bow;
But this said the other archers,
That it came from Walter's bow.
It appeared so, for he fled straightaway.
He escaped, the king fell.
25 Four times he cried out.
He asked for the sacrament,
But there was no one to give it him.
Far from any minster was he, in a waste;

But yet a hunter
30   Took some herbs with all their flower,
He made the king eat a little;
Thus he thought to communicate him.
He was in God and ought to be.
He had taken consecrated bread
35 ·   The Sunday before.
This should be a good warrant for him.

★   ★   ★

Then might you see barons on foot
Go weeping and sad.
They would not ride
40   Because of their lord whom they held so dear.
And the grooms went after
Weeping, and much they bewailed themselves.
The hunters all together
Said, "Wretched, miserable,
45   "What shall we do? What will become of us?
"Never shall we have such a lord."
Till Winchester they did not stop.
There they placed the king
Within the minster of St. Swithun.
50   There the barons assembled,
With the clergy of the city,
And the bishop and the abbot.
The good bishop Walkelin
Watched the king till morning;
55   With him monks, clerks, and abbots.
Well was he served and sung for.
Next day was such a dole
As never man saw in his life;
Nor so many masses, nor such service
60   Will be done, till God come to judgement,
For one king alone, as they did for him.
Quite otherwise they buried him
Than the barons had done
Where Walter shot him
Lestoire des Engles solum La Translacion Maistre Geffrei Gaimar,
eds T. Duff Hardy and C. T. Martin (2 vols, Rolls Series,
London, H.M.S.O., 1888–9), vol II, pp 199–203

Questions

a   What does this account add to what the other extracts have told
us about Tirel's part in Rufus' death?

b How does this extract differ from extracts *b* and *c* in its account of people's reactions to Rufus' death?

c Consult extracts *b*, *c*, *d* and *f*. Compare the writers' opinions of Rufus' attitude to religion.

d Why might this extract *f* be less reliable than some of the other extracts we have examined?

e What evidence exists in the extracts to suggest that Henry deliberately plotted his brother's death?

f Why, on the basis of the evidence presented in these six extracts, would it be difficult to decide whether or not the king's death was accidental?

You can compare your answer with a recent historian's verdict in extract *g*.

7   An historian's verdict

(g) It is clear that there is only one story, and that this, even with the minor variations introduced by the several retailers, is no more than a bare outline. The king, contrary to his usual custom, did not go hunting at dawn but waited until after the midday meal: perhaps he
5 had a hangover or was detained by important business; possibly he was held up by warnings of danger to his person.

The method of hunting envisaged, but never explicitly described, by those who wanted to explain how the accident occurred, was shooting dismounted from butts or trysts at animals driven by the
10 huntsmen through the glades in the wood where the royal party was stationed, split up into small groups at some distance from one another. The king was killed accidentally; but since his companion, Walter Tirel, fled, apparently without offering an explanation, and those in attendance may not have seen what happened, the precise
15 circumstances remained a mystery. And, as it was long before the age when writers constructed ingenious plots, no one looked further than the obvious suspect, and no one considered who benefitted by the death. There are no dark hints of earthy crime in the accounts already discussed. When such an evident sinner perished, there was
20 no need at all to look beyond the avenging hand of God.

F. Barlow, *William Rufus* (London, Methuen, 1983), p 425

VI   The Rule of Henry I

Introduction

No English king in a reign of comparable length has left so faint an imprint on the popular imagination or even on the minds of students of history as Henry I. 'Yet,' as Sir Richard Southern has said, 'the materials for his reign are neither scarce nor unexciting; they are more varied than for any previous period, and, they tell a story of new beginnings in many fields.' It is remarkable, therefore, that no full-length study of Henry I has been produced by an historian, although one by C. W. Hollister is promised shortly. The lack of a major history of Henry's reign makes assessment of his rule difficult, for the traditional view of his reign has been much coloured by Angevin historiography which sought to portray Stephen's reign as an unfortunate period of misery between the periods of stability provided by the first two Henrys. This view is reflected in the textbooks of both the nineteenth and twentieth centuries. According to Bishop Stubbs, Henry 'was . . . a strong ruler, with a clear view of his own interests, methodical, sagacious and far sighted: his selfish aims dictated the policy that gave peace and order to his people: destroying his enemies, he destroyed theirs; and by enforcing order he paved the way for law. Such a king neither expects nor deserves love; but he is regarded with a mixed feeling of confidence and awe, and the result of his rule is better than that of many who are called benefactors.' H. G. Richardson and G. O. Sayles, savage critics of much of Stubbs' work, were still able to regard Henry I as one of the two men 'of outstanding genius' that the Normans produced in the twelfth century. (The other was Roger of Salisbury.) Henry's reputation is maintained in what is probably the 'standard' textbook used by sixth-formers and undergraduates working on Norman England today, Frank Barlow's *The Feudal Kingdom of England 1042–1216*: 'With the reign of Henry I', declares Professor Barlow, 'Norman kingship reached its splendid apogee in England. With the reign of Stephen . . . it fell to its lowest level.'

However, there is room for more shades of grey than these bold strokes indicate. A. L. Poole's assessment of Henry's reign, published in 1951, is much more cautious. Henry, Poole argued, did little more than hold his own in the political sphere. He failed to establish durable peace, he ruled arbitrarily, and much of the blame for the problems of Stephen's reign, should be placed on Henry's premature and over-rigid centralization. Nevertheless, Henry's reputation has remained high and was indeed increased by Sir Richard Southern's suggestive analysis of Henry's place in English history. Not least, Southern argued that Henry's reign was especially significant for the use Henry made of royal patronage as an instrument of government. Henry was not a creator of institutions, but he did insert into the social fabric men who had a direct interest in royal government and who depended on royal government for their rise and on its continuance for their survival. In short, in Southern's view, Henry was a master of the art of government.

Since the publication of Southern's lecture much work has been done by historians on Henry's reign. Some of it, in journals like *History* and the *English Historical Review* perhaps comes to the attention of the keen sixth-former, but much of this new work is published in journals like *Speculum*, *Viator*, *Albion* and the *American Historical Review* which are unavailable to most schools. Much of this work is detailed and technical, based on the earliest surviving Pipe Roll or on the charters of Henry's reign, but it will undoubtedly allow a much more accurate understanding of how Henry's government actually worked.

The aim of this unit, then, is to try to raise some questions about the nature of Henry's rule. How secure was it? What role did patronage play in it? Was Henry an arbitrary ruler whose strength lay in his ruthlessness and determination? Did Henry's treatment of the established nobility differ from his treatment of his 'new men'? Is, indeed, the concept of 'new men' valid in a society so recently established by conquest?

It is still easier to ask these questions, than to provide answers to them. But in all arguments about the 'success' and 'efficiency' of medieval governments – or, indeed, any government – it is worth bearing in mind an awareness of the limitations of government's power. What sort of control could a medieval government realistically be expected to possess, given the bureaucratic and technological strengths and weaknesses it had?

Further Reading

R. W. Southern's seminal article 'The Place of Henry I in English History' is most easily found in his *Medieval Humanism and Other Studies* (Oxford, Blackwell, 1970). W. Stubbs, *The Constitutional History of England* (3rd edn, Oxford, Clarendon Press, 1880) and H. G. Richardson and G. O. Sayles, *The Governance of Medieval England* (Edinburgh U.P., 1963) should be consulted by those keen to probe more deeply into Henry's reign. F. Barlow, *The Feudal Kingdom of England, 1042–1216* (3rd edn, London, Longman, 1972), A. L. Poole, *From Domesday Book to Magna Carta, 1087–1216* (Oxford, O.U.P., 1951) and M. T. Clanchy, *England and its Rulers, 1066–1272* (Glasgow, Fontana, 1983) are all essential.

1   The Anglo-Saxon Chronicle's view of Henry I

(a) 1118. All this year King Henry stayed in Normandy because of the war with the king of France and the count of Anjou and the count of Flanders. Because of these hostilities the king was much distressed and lost a great deal both in money and also in land, and the people
5   who troubled him most were his own men, who frequently deserted him and betrayed him and went over to his enemies, and gave their castles up to them for the injury and betrayal of the king. England paid dear for all this, because of the various taxes that never ceased in the course of all this year.

10   (b) 1125. In this year King Henry sent to England from Normandy before Christmas, and ordered that all the moneyers who were in England should be mutilated – i.e. that each should lose the right hand and be castrated. That was because the man who had a pound could not get a pennyworth at a market. And Bishop Roger of
15   Salisbury sent over all England and ordered them all to come to Winchester at Christmas. When they got there, they were taken one by one and each deprived of the right hand, and castrated. All this was done before Twelfth Night, and it was done very justly because they had ruined all the country with their great false-dealing: they all
20   paid for it.

(c) 1135 . . . for that same year the king died the day after St. Andrew's Day, in Normandy. Then forthwith these lands grew dark, for everyone who could forthwith robbed another . . . He (Henry) was a good man, and people were in great awe of him. No
25   one dared injure another in his time. He made peace for man and beast. Whoever carried his burden of gold and silver nobody dared say anything but good to him.

> *The Anglo-Saxon Chronicle*, trans. G. N. Garmonsway (London, Dent, 1953), pp 247–63

Questions

* *a* Consult extract *a*. What types of taxes did Henry raise in England to pay for his wars in Normandy (line 8)?
  b Consult extract *b*. What were 'moneyers' (line 11)? What offence had the moneyers committed?
  c Consult extracts *a*, *b* and *c*. How successfully did the chronicler think that Henry governed England?

2   A French view of Henry I in 1118

(a) Meanwhile the king of England prepared in great haste to build a castle: he spurred on his labourers, while king Louis left his own castle after providing it with a garrison of knights. Henry had his

castle built on the nearest high ground, so that with numerous
5 knights and the covering fire of his crossbowmen and archers he
could cut his enemies' supply lines from his own territory. He could
tie them down and sow confusion amongst them. But the king of
France, returning blow for blow, was not slow to get his own back,
so astute was he. He reassembled an army and returning suddenly at
10 dawn attacked courageously the new castle which the local people
had named Malassis. With tremendous efforts, and despite heavy
losses on both sides, Louis destroyed Henry's castle, and to the glory
of the kingdom and the shame of his opponent, he scattered with
true valour all the plots attacked against him.

15 On the other hand, since Fortune, in her power, spares no-one,
the king of England, after long and admirable successes in the most
peaceful prosperity, fell from the pinnacle of the wheel of fortune
and saw himself subjected to the changing and unfortunate
vicissitudes of events. Alongside the king of France, the Count of
20 Flanders and Fulk, Count of Angers deployed all their strength to
trouble and to attack Henry. And he did not face trouble from
abroad only, but also internally, from amongst his own men,
namely Hugh of Gournay, the Count of Eu, the Count of Aumales
and several others, who waged war against him.

25 As a crowning misfortune, he suffered difficulties that wicked
men created for him in his household. Dreading the secret factions of
his household servants and chamberlains, he continually changed his
bed and kept increasing his armed guards because of his fear of the
night. Every night before he slept he had laid out for him a shield and
30 a sword. One of these conspirators, named H., who was one of his
closest friends, enriched by royal generosity, was caught in the act of
plotting and was condemned to be blinded and castrated; a merciful
sentence, for he deserved the rope. In such conditions, there was no
security at all for the king. Henry, whose natural magnanimity and
35 courage were well known, took paltry precautions. Even in his
house, he kept his sword buckled on. He did not allow those whom
he considered the most loyal of his servants to go about their
business without their swords, and that on pain of a fine which he
fixed at an arbitrary figure, as in a game.

Adapted from Suger, *Vie de Louis VI le Gros*, ed. et trad. Henri
Waquet (Paris, Société d'Edition, 'Les Belles Lettres', 1964),
pp 188–91

Questions

a   How would you assess the attitude of Suger towards Henry?
★ b   Where did Hugh of Gournay, the Count of Eu and the Count of
     Aumales make trouble for Henry?

3 Three views of Henry's good government

(a) Henry, the youngest son of William the Great, was born in England in the third year after his father's coming to this country. He was a child who enjoyed the ardent good wishes of all, for to him the kingdom seemed to pertain as of right since he was the only one of
5 William's sons who was born when his father was a king. He was early instructed in the liberal arts . . . he learnt by degrees how to restrain the people with mercifulness, and only to employ his troops when there was a pressing emergency . . .

On the violent death of King William after the solemnisation of
10 the royal funeral he was chosen king, though some small dissension had arisen among the magnates which was allayed mainly by the exertions of Henry, earl of Warwick, a man of unblemished integrity with whom he had long been in the closest intimacy. He immediately issued an edict throughout England annulling the
15 illegal practices of his brother and of Rannulf. He remitted taxes, released prisoners, drove the unnaturally vicious from the court, and restored the nightly use of lights within the palace which in his brother's time had been discontinued. He renewed the operation of the ancient laws, confirming them with his own oath, and that of the
20 magnates so that they should not be evaded. A joyful day then seemed to dawn upon the people when the light of fair promise shone forth after such repeated clouds of distress. And that nothing might be wanting in the universal joy, Rannulf, that sink of iniquity, was cast into prison and speedy messengers were sent to recall
25 Anselm. So amid universal rejoicing Henry was crowned king at London on 5 August, that is to say, four days after his brother's death. These acts were the more carefully carried out lest the magnates should be induced to repent their choice, as a rumour prevailed that Robert, count of Normandy, was about to arrive
30 home on his return from Apulia. Soon afterwards the friends of the king and particularly the bishops persuaded him to give up his pleasure in mistresses, and to take a lawful wife. Therefore, on 11 November he married Maud, daughter of Malcolm, king of Scots, for whom he had been greatly attached. He little regarded the
35 marriage portion if he could possess her whom he so ardently desired. For though she was of noble descent, being grand-niece of King Edward by his brother Edmund, yet she possessed but little fortune, being an orphan deprived of both parents . . . (Henry) was active in providing what conduced to the strength of his dominion,
40 and firm in defending it. He refrained from war so long as he could do so with honour, but when he resorted to arms he was a most severe requiter of injuries, dispelling anger by his energy and courage. He was constant alike in his enmities and in his general benevolence, giving too much rein to his anger in the one case and
45 displaying his royal magnanimity in the other. For he reduced his

enemies even to ruin, and he exalted his friends and dependants so that all men envied them . . .

Rebellions among his nobles never caused him to be treacherously attacked by his attendants, save only once when a certain
50 chamberlain of humble birth, but distinguished as the keeper of the king's treasure, was detected in such an attempt, and, after confession suffered a bitter penalty. With this exception the king remained secure throughout his life: fear restrained the minds of all and admiration controlled their conversation.

Adapted from William of Malmesbury, *De Gesta Regum*, as translated in *English Historical Documents II 1042–1189* (2nd edn, London, Eyre and Spottiswoode, 1981), pp 319–21

Questions

a   How can this document be used to support the view that Henry was able to use a claim of porphyrogeniture in his efforts to secure the throne of England?
★ b   What was 'the edict' (line 14) issued by Henry and what was its main purpose?
★ c   Who was the 'Rannulf' referred to in the document? Why was it advantageous to Henry to treat him harshly? What happened to Rannulf in Henry's reign?
d   What reasons might Henry have had for marrying Maud if she was not wealthy?
e   Compare the final paragraph of this extract with the previous extract from Suger's *Life of Louis VI*. How differently do the two writers treat Henry's fears of disloyalty?

(b) So King Henry with God's aid brought all his enemies low, and demolished the unlicensed castles that Robert and the factious lords had built. For fear that dissidents might molest simple and peaceful folk under the pretext of helping his brother, he sent him to England
5 and kept him for twenty-seven years in prison, providing him liberally with every comfort. During this time he himself governed the duchy of Normandy firmly together with the kingdom of England; up to the end of his life he always devoted himself to preserving peace, and after he had secured the lasting prosperity he
10 desired he never declined from his early power and strict justice. He shrewdly kept down illustrious counts and castellans and bold tyrants to prevent seditious uprisings, but always cared for and protected men of peace and monks and the humble people. After becoming firmly established in his government on both sides of the
15 Channel in the eighth year of his reign, he always attempted to give peace to his subject peoples, and strictly punished law-breakers according to severe laws. Possessing an abundance of wealth and luxuries, he gave way too easily to the sin of lust; from boyhood

until old age he was sinfully enslaved by this vice and had many sons
20 and daughters by his mistresses. A man of tremendous energy, he
greatly increased his wordly possessions, and collected a huge
treasure-store of precious objects. He claimed for himself alone the
hunting rights all over England, and even had the feet of dogs living
in the neighbourhood of forests mutilated, only grudgingly
25 allowing a few of his greatest nobles and closest friends the privilege
of hunting in their own woods. A diligent investigator, he inquired
into everything, and retained all the business of officials and
dignitaries; and, since he was an assiduous ruler, kept an eye on the
many happenings in England and Normandy. He was thoroughly
30 familiar with all secrets and things done surreptitiously, so that their
perpetrators could not imagine how the king could be aware of their
most secret plots. After thorough study of past histories, I
confidently assert that no king in the English realm was ever more
richly or powerfully equipped than Henry in everything that
35 contributes to worldly glory.

> The Ecclesiastical History of Orderic Vitalis, ed. Marjorie
> Chibnall (6 vols, Oxford, O.U.P., 1969–80), vol VI,
> pp 98–101

Questions

★ *a* To what events is Orderic referring at the beginning of this
extract (lines 1–3)?
★ *b* Does Henry deserve Orderic's praise of his wealth gathering?
★ *c* How did Henry claim and enforce 'the hunting rights all over
England' (lines 22–23)?

(c) On the death of the great King Henry, his character was freely
canvassed by the people, as is usual, after men are dead. Some
contended that he was eminently distinguished for three brilliant
gifts. These were, great sagacity, for his counsels were profound, his
5 foresight keen, and his eloquence commanding; success in war, for,
besides other splendid achievements, he was victorious over the king
of France; and wealth, in which he far surpassed all his predecessors.
Others, however, taking a different view attributed to him three
gross vices: avarice, as, though his wealth was great, in imitation of
10 his progenitors he impoverished the people by taxes and exactions,
entangling them in the toils of informers; cruelty in that he plucked
out the eyes of his kinsman, the Earl of Morton, in his captivity,
though the horrid deed was unknown until death revealed the king's
secrets: and they mentioned other instances of which I will say
15 nothing; and wantonness, for, like Solomon, he was perpetually
enslaved by female seductions. Such remarks were freely bruited
abroad. But in the troublesome times succeeded from the atrocities
of the Normans, whatever King Henry had done, either

despotically, or in the regular exercise of his royal authority,
20 appeared in comparison most excellent.

The Chronicle of Henry of Huntingdon, trans. and ed. T.
Forester (London, Henry G. Bohn, 1853), pp 261–2

Questions

★ a On what occasions was Henry 'victorious over the king of
France' (lines 6–7)?

★ b When and why did Henry ill-treat the Earl of Morton?

   c Why were Orderic and Henry of Huntingdon so concerned
about Henry's sexual proclivities?

   d Compare Henry of Huntingdon's attitude to Henry's cruelty
with the attitudes expressed in *The Anglo-Saxon Chronicle* (p 65)
and in Suger's *Life of Louis VI* (pp 65–6).

   e How could extract *c* be used to argue that Henry's rule was not
completely secure from the threat of serious opposition?

   f Compare the different assessments of Henry that you have read
so far. How far do they agree and disagree?

   g Using the information you have gathered so far, write your own
character study of Henry.

4 New men and established magnates

(a) He brought all his enemies to heel by his wisdom and courage,
and rewarded his loyal supporters with riches and honours. So he
pulled down many great men from positions of eminence for their
presumption, and sentenced them to be disinherited for ever. On the
5 other hand, he ennobled others of base stock who had served him
well, raised them, so to say, from the dust, and heaping all kinds of
favours on them, stationed them above earls and famous castellans.
Witnesses of the truth of my words are Geoffrey of Clinton, Ralph
Basset, Hugh of Buckland, Guillegrip, Rainer of Bath, William
10 Trussebut, Haimo of Falaise, Guigan Algason, Robert of Bostare,
and many others, who have heaped up riches and built lavishly, on a
scale far beyond the means of their fathers; witnesses too are the men
who, on trumped-up and unjust pretexts, have been oppressed by
them. The king raised to high rank all these and many others of low
15 birth whom it would be tedious to name individually, lifted them
out of insignificance by his royal authority, set them on the summit
of power, and made them formidable even to the greatest magnates
of the kingdom.

The Ecclesiastical History of Orderic Vitalis, ed. Marjorie
Chibnall (6 vols, Oxford, O.U.P., 1969–80), vol VI,
pp 16–17

(b) From the beginning of his reign Henry wisely recommended

20　himself to all men, inviting them into his favour with royal gifts. He
　　treated the magnates with honour and generosity, adding to their
　　wealth and estates, and by placating them in this way won their
　　loyalty. He helped his humble subjects by giving just laws, and
　　protected them by his patronage from unjust extortions and
25　robbers . . .
　　　He began to provide the widowed church with pastors, and on the
　　advice of his senior counsellors placed learned scholars in them. He
　　made William Gifford, who had been the dead king's chancellor,
　　bishop of Winchester, and promoted Gerard, bishop of Hereford, to
30　be archbishop of York. He sent speedy messengers across the
　　Channel to invite back to his see the venerable Anselm, archbishop
　　of Canterbury . . . He gave the abbey of Ely to Richard the son of
　　Richard of Bienfaite, a monk of Bec, and the abbey of Bury St.
　　Edmunds to Robert, a young monk of Saint-Evroul, the son of
35　Hugh, earl of Chester. Glastonbury he entrusted to Herluin of Caen,
　　and Abingdon to Faricius of Malmesbury.
　　　When Hugh, earl of Chester, and Robert of Bellême and other
　　magnates who were in Normandy heard of the death of the
　　unfortunate king and the sudden revolution, they settled their affairs
40　in Normandy and hurried back to England, where they dutifully
　　submitted to the new king and, after doing homage, received their
　　estates and all their dignities from him, together with royal gifts.
　　　King Henry did not follow the advice of rash young men as
　　Rehoboam did, but prudently took to heart the experience and
45　advice of wise and older men. He summoned to his counsels Robert
　　of Meulan and Hugh of Chester, Richard of Reviers and Roger
　　Bigod, and other active and able men. Because he humbly deferred
　　to men of experience he deservedly governed many provinces and
　　peoples.

> *The Ecclesiastical History of Orderic Vitalis*, ed. Marjorie
> Chibnall (6 vols, Oxford, O.U.P., 1969–80), vol V, pp 296–
> 299

50　(c) Robert, count of Meulan . . . said to the king (in the autumn of
　　1101 shortly after Robert, duke of Normandy had landed in
　　England) "Every brave man who has aspired to knighthood and sees
　　his friend hard pressed in the mêlée ought, if he wishes to be thought
　　worthy of his standing, to go to that friend's help in his need as best
55　he may. In such a cause one should think not so much of future
　　reward as of rescuing the friend who needs one. Now indeed we see
　　many acting in a very different way, and besmirching by shameful
　　prevarication the bright faith they have pledged to their lord. Such
　　things are plain for us to see and we feel the sharp stabs in our sides.
60　We, therefore, who have been entrusted by God to provide for the
　　common good ought to keep a sharp look-out to preserve the safety
　　of the realm and of the Church of God. Let our chief care be to

triumph peacefully by God's grace and win a victory without shedding Christian blood, so that our loyal people may enjoy the
65 security of peace. Now, therefore, hear my counsel, my lord king, and do not scorn to follow my advice. Speak to all your knights with moderation; coax them as a father would his sons, placate every one with promises, grant whatever they ask, and in this way draw all men assiduously to your cause. If they ask for London or York, do
70 not hesitate to promise great rewards appropriate to royal munificence. It is better to give a small part of the kingdom than to sacrifice victory and life itself to a host of enemies. When with God's help we come safely to the end of this business we will propose practical measures for recovering the demesnes appropriated by rash
75 deserters in a time of war. There is no doubt that anyone who chooses to desert his lord in an hour of deadly danger and seeks another lord for greed of gain, or insists on payment for the military service that he ought to offer freely to his king for the defence of the realm, and attempts to deprive him of his own demesnes will be
80 judged a traitor by a just and equitable judgement, and will rightly be deprived of his inheritance and forced to flee the country."

All the magnates who were with King Henry applauded the count's speech and urged the king to follow his advice. Being a man of remarkable sagacity, he thanked the counsellors who wished him
85 well and readily accepted their practical suggestions, winning with promises and gifts the support of many whom he regarded with suspicion.

> The Ecclesiastical History of Orderic Vitalis, ed. Marjorie Chibnall (6 vols, Oxford, O.U.P., 1969–80), vol V, pp 314–317

Questions

★ a What do you understand by the word 'honour' (extract *a* line 2)?
★ b Trace the careers of Geoffrey of Clinton and Ralph Bassett. Do their careers bear out Orderic's words that they were 'raised . . . from the dust' (line 6)?
★ c Define the terms 'magnate' and 'new man'.
★ d Why does Orderic describe the church as 'widowed' (extract *b* line 26)?
★ e What happened to Robert of Bellême in Henry's reign?
★ f How was the conflict between Henry and Robert of Normandy resolved in 1101?
   g Compare the three extracts and assess how Henry dealt with the problem of patronage in them.

5 Government in action

(a) Henry, king of the English, to Samson (Bishop of Worcester, 1096–1112) . . . and to all the barons of Worcestershire, both French

and English, greeting. Know that I grant and order that henceforth
my shire courts and hundred courts shall meet in the same places and
5 at the same terms as they were wont to do in the time of King
Edward (the Confessor), and not otherwise. And I do not wish that
my sheriff should make them assemble in different fashion because
of his own needs or interests. For I myself, if ever I shall wish it, will
cause them to be summoned at my own pleasure, if it be necessary
10 for my royal interests. And if in the future there should arise a
dispute concerning the allotment of land, or concerning its seizure,
let this be tried in my own court if it be between my tenants-in-chief.
But if the dispute be between the vassals of two different lords let the
plea be held in the shire court; and if it be not there settled, let the
15 matter be decided by the duel. And I will and order that the men of
the shire so attend the meetings of the shire courts and hundred
courts as they were wont to do in the time of King Edward; nor may
anyone claim excuse or quittance from me from following my pleas
and my judgements as they then did.

> Charter of Henry I concerning the holding of the courts of the
> shire and hundred (26 July 1108–August 1111), in *English
> Historical Documents II 1042–1189* (2nd edn, London, Eyre
> and Spottiswoode, 1981), p 465

Questions

★ a What sorts of problems did shire and hundred courts deal with?
★ b What problem for royal administration is Henry trying to
   counteract here?
★ c What does the phrase 'let the matter be decided by the duel' (lines
   14–15) mean?
★ d What does the term 'quittance' (line 18) mean?
  e Read the following short writ issued in the reign of Edward the
   Confessor:

20 Edward the king to Grimketel (Bishop of Selsey 1039–47) . . . and
all my thegns in Suffolk, greeting. I make known to you that I will
that the soke of the eight and a half hundreds that pertains to Thingow
shall be held . . . by St. Edmund with sake and soke (rights of
jurisdiction) as fully as my mother held it. And I forbid that any man
25 shall take away anything that I have already given her.

> *English Historical Documents II 1042–1189* (2nd edn, London,
> Eyre and Spottiswoode, 1981), p 460

The two writs printed in this section are not atypical of the reigns
of Henry I and Edward the Confessor. Is it possible to discern
any difference in the tone of the language of the two writs? If
there is a difference in tone, what significance do you think it has?

(b) 2. If any of my barons or of my earls or any other of my tenants

shall die, his heir shall not redeem his land as he wont to do in the time of my brother, but he shall henceforth redeem it by means of a just and lawful 'relief'. Similarly the men of my barons shall redeem
30 their lands from their lords by means of a just and lawful relief.

3. If any of my barons or my tenants shall wish to give in marriage his daughter or his sister or his niece or his cousin, he shall consult me about the matter; but I will neither seek payment for my consent, nor will I refuse my permission, unless he wishes to give her in marriage
35 to one of my enemies. And if, on the death of one of my barons or one of my tenants, a daughter should be his heir, I will dispose of her in marriage and of her lands according to the counsel given me by my barons. And if the wife of one of my tenants shall survive her husband and be without children she shall have her dower and her
40 marriage portion, and I will not give her in marriage unless she herself consents.

4. If a widow survives with children under age, she shall have her dower and her marriage portion, so long as she keeps her body chaste; and I will not give her in marriage except with her consent.
45 And the guardian of the land, and of the children shall be either the widow or another of their relations, as may seem more proper. And I order that my barons shall act likewise towards the sons and daughters and widows of their men.

From Henry I's Coronation Charter in *English Historical Documents II 1042–1189* (2nd edn, London, Eyre and Spottiswoode, 1981), p 433

Questions

* *a*   What was a 'relief' (line 29)?
* *b*   What were 'dowers' and 'marriage portions' (lines 39–40)?
  c   Why did Henry issue this document?

(c)Lincolnshire
50 Earl Rannulf of Chester owes 1000 pounds for the debt of his father for the land of his father, earl Hugh.

Essex
Geoffrey de Mandeville accounts for £866 13s 4d for the land of his father. He has paid £133 6s 8d in the treasury.

55 Hampshire
And the same sheriff (William de Pontlearch) owes £100 3 gold marks for the custody of the land of Walter, son of Uluric Venator, until his heir could take possession of it.

Lincolnshire
60 Robert of . . . accounts for 30 silver marks for the relief of his

father's land. He has paid £8 6s 8d in the treasury. And he owes £11 13s 4d.

Robert Marmion accounts for £176 13s 4d for the relief of his father's land. He has paid £60 in the treasury. And he owes £116 13s 65 4d.

Walter of . . . accounts for £98 3s so that he can possess the land of William of Alost as his own fief. He had paid 50 silver marks in the treasury. And he owes £64 15s 4d.

Lucy, Countess of Chester accounts for £266 13s 4d for the land of 70 her father. She has paid £166 13s 4d in the treasury. And she owes £100, and 500 silver marks so that she does not have to take a husband in the next five years.

Extracts from *Magnum Rotulum Scaccarii vel Magnum Rotulum Pipae de Anno Tricesimo – Primo Regni Henrici Primi* (Pipe Roll of 31 Henry I), ed. J. Hunter (London, Record Commission, 1833), pp 110, 55, 37, 83, 111, 110

Questions

a   What do the extracts from the Pipe Roll suggest about Henry's promise in clause 2 of the Coronation Charter?
b   What does the final extract from the Pipe Roll (lines 69–72) suggest about Henry's promise in clause 4 of the Coronation Charter?
★   c   What was the Pipe Roll? Explain its place in Henry I's financial system.
d   What conclusions could you draw about the nature of royal power in England in c. 1130 by comparing the extracts from the Coronation Charter with the extracts from the Pipe Roll?

6   Some modern statistics from the Pipe Roll of 31 Henry I

(a) Items datable to 1129–30
The table on page 76 records accounts arising in 1129–30 only. Column I lists the amounts demanded by the Board of Exchequer. Column II indicates the amounts paid in by the Sheriff, while Column III lists the amounts pardoned. Column IV indicates the expenditure incurred by the Sheriff, and Column V indicates what is still owed on the original total demanded.

Questions

★   a   What were 'farms' (Items of revenue column)?
★   b   What was 'cornage'?

Item of revenue	I Total demanded	II Amount paid	III Amount pardoned	IV Expenditure	V Amount owing
County farms	9166 15 3	6343 1 0	87 9 9	804 15 10	1931 9 11
Estates in hand	2707 8 6	2232 12 6	1 3 0	193 18 6	280 4 6
Borough farms	360 11 2½	242 5 1	0 0 0	83 8 3½	34 17 10
Cornage, geld of animals	238 14 1½	156 12 3	1 17 4	42 7 7½	37 16 11
Danegeld	4355 12 7	2374 12 11	1810 17 1	0 0 0	170 2 7
Aids of boroughs, cities and counties	553 1 8	358 10 9	172 13 1	12 6 0	9 11 2
Aids of knights	58 6 8	45 16 8	0 0 0	0 0 0	12 10 0
Dona regis	0 0 0	0 0 0	0 0 0	0 0 0	0 0 0
Regalian rights	798 3 10	587 0 4	35 0 0	63 2 6	113 1 0
Forest revenues, other than pleas	149 8 2	110 3 4	13 0 1	15 5 2	13 6 11
Total	18,388 2 0	12,450 14 10	2,122 0 4	1,215 3 11	2,603 0 10

Figures are expressed in £ s d.

Table One of J. A. Green, 'The Earliest Surviving Pipe Roll', *Bulletin of Institute of Historical Research*, vol LV (University of London, 1982). p 15

*   c   How was 'danegeld' assessed?
    d   Why do you think so much danegeld was pardoned?
    e   Why do you think so much money went uncollected?

(b) Recipients of royal patronage according to the value of their exemptions, gifts and pardons

Value per individual	Number of individuals	Total value
£50–318	18 (3.0%)	£2,223 (51.0%)
£6– 50	122 (15.5%)	£1,372 (31.5%)
£0– 6	526 (81.5%)	£761 (17.5%)

Appendix A, Part I of S. L. Mooers, 'Patronage in the Pipe Roll of 1130', *Speculum*, vol LIX (Medieval Academy of America, Cambridge, Mass., 1984), p 305. The first column indicates the range of value of the patronage received in the form of exemptions from taxes and duties, gifts and pardons. The second lists the number of individuals who received patronage of a particular value, and the third column indicates the total value of patronage received by all the individuals in that particular range of patronage.

Questions

a   What conclusions can you draw from the table about the way in which Henry I's patronage was distributed?
b   Do you think that the distribution of patronage showed the strength or the weakness of the crown?

VII   The Reign of Stephen

Introduction

Unlike Henry I, Stephen has much more frequently attracted the attention of historians. Most, however, come to castigate rather than admire him. F. M. Stenton considered Stephen largely responsible for his own failure, for 'he was obviously incapable of following out a long course of consistent action, and there is no sign that he so much as understood the meaning of policy'. A. L. Poole believed that Stephen made foolish concessions through his indecisiveness and incompetence. More recent studies are no less unflattering. To R. H. C. Davis, Stephen was 'a man of great activity but little judgement'. He was 'an excellent warrior' but he often failed to complete what he set out to do. 'Basically small-minded' Stephen had no chance of solving the problems he faced in 1135.

The result of Stephen's accession was civil war and, in many historians' eyes, anarchy. The parameters of this approach to Stephen's reign were established by the very famous book by J. H. Round on Geoffrey de Mandeville, which bore the telling subtitle, 'A Study of Anarchy'. Round was actually sympathetic to the problems which Stephen faced, but his characterisation of Geoffrey de Mandeville has long dominated the popular view of Stephen's reign. Geoffrey was, according to Round, 'the most perfect and typical presentment of the feudal and anarchic spirit that stamps the reign of Stephen'. More recently, some historians have questioned whether what happened in Stephen's reign was 'anarchy' or not. The barons, they argue, were not reacting blindly against the constraints imposed upon them by the harshness of the rule of Henry I, but were seeking instead to establish their hereditary rights which they felt had been treated with undue disregard. Even so, the latest full-length study of Stephen's reign by an academic historian, H. A. Cronne, bears the title *The Reign of Stephen 1135–54: Anarchy in England*, although the author very quickly remarks that 'Anarchical conditions . . . were neither universal nor continuous in England as a whole and there were even some regions such as Kent which saw little fighting and suffered relatively speaking, very lightly'. On the other hand, C. W. Hollister has argued since then in the American journal *Albion* that, despite the doubts raised by some historians, 'Stephen's anarchy is a venerable concept and an apt one'.

Anarchy or not, civil war did occur in Stephen's reign. Why it occurred is, of course, a fascinating but intensely problematical question. Numerous circumstances might have some bearing on the origins of the war. Stephen's reign saw a remarkable flourishing of intellectual activity in England in, for example, the work of John of Salisbury, Gilbert Foliot and the household of Theobald, archbishop of Canterbury. It is possible, then, that ideas entered the conflict in England. While there were regional variations in economic prosperity in Henry I's time, prosperity seems to have outweighed depression. Could it be that economic prosperity led to political instability? Was Henry I's government less secure and powerful than most historians have assumed? It is, of course, possible that Stephen's reign was less of a departure from the normality of the twelfth century than we generally assume.

Although we can only touch on such wide-ranging questions indirectly in this unit, it is important to keep them in mind when attempting to make an overall assessment of Stephen's reign. They might affect the arguments raised by consideration of seemingly more compact problems too. Why was Stephen so readily accepted in 1135–6 despite the promises of many barons made to Henry I about Matilda? Why does it take nearly four years for the succession dispute to come out into the open? Could it be that the civil war caused the succession dispute, rather than the more prosaic pattern of causation – of succession dispute leading to civil war? Why were the leading bishops arrested in 1139 after their apparently loyal service to Stephen since Henry's death?

The war against the Angevins and the internecine struggles in England in the 1140s followed a tortuous course. Questions about them abound. Was the conflict superficial or did it have important consequences for the English economy or the pattern of land ownership? Why did Matilda fail to control England in 1141 after Stephen's capture at Lincoln? The termination of the conflict is also remarkable. It might throw light on the nature of the earlier wars. Central to all these questions is the nature of Stephen's character. Might its alleged weakness largely explain the difficulties of the reign?

Stephen's reign might have received a lot of attention from academic historians, but much remains uncertain and much remains to be done on the sources that have survived. It is hoped that, as in all the other sections of this book, the documents used and the questions raised here will stimulate the reader to research more widely in both the secondary and primary materials in order to gain a deeper understanding of this king who, a late twelfth-century chronicler, Gervase of Canterbury, remarked was accustomed 'to start many endeavours with vigour, but to bring few to a praiseworthy end'.

Further Reading

The relevant sections of M. T. Clanchy, *England and its Rulers,*

1066–1272 (Glasgow, Fontana, 1983) and F. Barlow, *The Feudal Kingdom of England, 1042–1216* (3rd edn, London, Longman, 1972) are the best starting places for work on Stephen. The works by J. H. Round and H. A. Cronne mentioned in the introduction are invaluable, as is R. H. C. Davis, *King Stephen* (London, Longman, 1967). Some of the more recent and valuable work on Stephen's reign is in article form. The motives of the barons in the conflicts are considered in J. C. Holt, 'Politics and Property in Early Medieval England', *Past and Present*, no 57 (1972), pp 3–52; J. Le Patourel, 'What did not happen in Stephen's reign', *History*, vol 58 (1973), pp 1–17; C. W. Hollister, 'The Misfortunes of the Mandevilles', *History*, vol 58 (1973), pp 18–28; E. King, 'King Stephen and the Anglo-Norman Aristocracy', *History*, vol 59 (1974), pp 180–94.

1   Getting the throne

(a) In 1135 Henry, the most illustrious king of England, and duke of Normandy, being dead, but not yet buried, Stephen of Boulogne, his nephew on the sister's side, seized on the kingdom of England. Stephen, the elder, count of Blois, had married the daughter of
5 William the first, a noble lady, and had issue by her four sons. The count dying in the East, his widow, in her wisdom, setting aside her eldest born, as he was indolent, and appeared to be of degenerate nature, exalted her favourite son, Theobald, to the entire inheritance; she sent Stephen, yet a lad, to the king his uncle, to be
10 educated and advanced; and that she might not seem to have borne children solely for secular purposes, she placed Henry, her fourth son, in the monastery at Clugny. In the process of time, king Henry gave the only daughter of the count of Boulogne, to whom the inheritance pertained, to his nephew Stephen in marriage,
15 bestowing upon him also large possessions in England. To his nephew Henry, a monk of Clugny, he likewise gave the abbey of Glastonbury, and, after a time, advanced him to the bishopric of Winchester. When, therefore, as already said, king Henry died, Stephen violating the oath, which he had sworn to king Henry's
20 daughter, of preserving his fidelity, seized upon the kingdom; and in this he was aided by the prelates and nobles who were bound by the same oath; William, archbishop of Canterbury, who had sworn first, then consecrated him king, with the help and assistance of Roger, bishop of Salisbury, who was the second who had sworn,
25 and had, moreover, administered the oath to every other individual. The archbishop, however, died in the very year of his apostasy, as a just punishment for his perjury, as it is believed. The bishop, too, ended his life, some years after, by a miserable death – the king himself becoming the minister of God's vengeance against him . . .
30 Stephen, therefore, in order that he might be elevated to the throne equally against both human and divine right – transgressing the one

by not being the legitimate heir, and the other by his perfidy –
promised everything which the prelates and nobles demanded: but
his want of faith rendered all these of no avail . . .

William of Newburgh, *Historia Rerum Anglicarum*, trans. in J.
Stevenson, *The Church Historians of England*, vol IV, Part II
(London, Seeleys, 1856), pp 408–9

35 (b) Meanwhile Stephen Count of Mortain & Boulogne, King
Henry's nephew . . . he who first among the laity, after the King of
Scots, had bound himself by allegiance to the Empress, hurried on
his arrival in England by way of Wissant. For certain reasons the
Empress and likewise her brother Robert Earl of Gloucester,
40 together with almost all the nobles, delayed their return to the
kingdom. Yet some castles in Normandy . . . sided with the heiress.
It is certainly established that on the day when Stephen landed in
England, at dawn, there was, contrary to the nature of winter in our
part of the world, a terrible sound of thunder accompanied by fearful
45 lightning, so that it was almost thought the world was breaking up.
On being received as king by the people of London and Winchester
he also brought over to his side Roger Bishop of Salisbury and
William de Pont de l'Arche, who had the charge of the royal
treasure. Nevertheless . . . all his efforts would have been in vain had
50 not his brother Henry Bishop of Winchester . . . granted him an easy
acquiescence, allowed indeed by a very strong hope that Stephen
would continue the way of his grandfather William in the
governance of the kingdom, especially as regards strict uprightness
in Church affairs. Wherefore the Bishop of Winchester made himself
55 guarantor and surety of the solemn oath that William Archbishop of
Canterbury exacted from Stephen about the restoration and
maintenance of the freedom of the Church . . . Stephen then was
crowned . . . in the presence of three bishops (the archbishop and
those of Winchester and Salisbury), no abbots and very few
60 nobles . . .

William of Malmesbury, *Historia Novella*, trans. K. R. Potter
(London, Nelson, 1955), pp 14–16

(c) So this great man (Stephen), as soon as he heard a report that
King Henry had breathed his last, forming a mighty design . . .
made for the coast, since he was the other side of the Channel, and
happening to gain a favourable wind turned his mind and his ship
65 towards England. And after landing with a very small retinue, he
journeyed hastily to London, the capital, the queen of the whole
kingdom. At his arrival the town was immediately filled with
excitement and came to meet him with acclamation, and whereas it
had been sadly mourning the grievous death of its protector Henry,
70 it revelled in exultant joy as though it had recovered him in Stephen.
So the elders and those most shrewd in counsel summoned an

assembly, and taking prudent forethought for the state of the kingdom, on their own initiative, they agreed unanimously to choose a king. For, they said, every kingdom was exposed to
75 calamities from ill-fortune when a representative of the whole government and a fount of justice was lacking. It was therefore worth their while to appoint as soon as possible a king who, with a view to re-establishing peace for the common benefit, would meet the insurgents of the kingdom in arms and would justly administer
80 the enactments of the laws. Moreover, they said, it was their right and peculiar privilege that if the king died from any cause a successor should immediately be appointed by their own choice; and they had no one at hand who could take the king's place and put an end to the great dangers threatening the kingdom except Stephen, who, they
85 thought, had been brought among them by Providence; all regarded him as suited to the position on account both of his high birth and good character. So, when these arguments had been heard and favourably received by all without any open objection, they made a degree in the commune admitting him to the sovereignty and
90 appointed him king with universal approval, though a mutual compact was previously made and an oath taken on both sides, as was commonly asserted, that as long as he lived the citizens would aid him with their resources and protect him with their power, while he would gird himself with all his might to pacify the kingdom for
95 the benefit of them all.

Gesta Stephani, ed. and trans. K. R. Potter (Oxford, Clarendon Press, 1976), pp 4–7

(d) William Archbishop of Canterbury . . . added that King Henry in his lifetime had bound the chief men of the whole kingdom with a most stringent oath not to recognize as their sovereign after his death anyone but his daughter whom he had married to the Count of
100 Anjou, or her heir, if an heir survived her; and therefore, he said, it was presumptuous to wish to desire anything contrary to this arrangement, especially as the king's daughter was still alive and was not deprived of the blessing of heirs.

To this the king's supporters gave a firm answer. 'It is true,' they
105 said, 'and not to be denied, that King Henry gave his daughter in marriage with a politic design, that he might establish peace more surely and securely between the Normans and the Angevins, who had often troubled each other from disputes. Also with that loud commanding utterance that nobody could resist he rather compelled
110 than directed the leading men of the whole kingdom to swear to accept her as his heir. And though he knew in advance that they swore unwillingly and that the oath would not be kept, still, like Ezelind, he wished to make peace in his own time and by one woman's marriage to weld together many thousands of men in
115 harmony. And that we might clearly recognize that he did not wish

what he had approved for a certain reason in his lifetime to remain unalterable after his death, in his death agony, with very many standing by – listening to his truthful confession of his errors, he very plainly showed repentance for the forcible imposition of the

120 oath on his barons. Wherefore, because it is acknowledged that any forcible exaction of an oath from anyone has made it impossible for the breaking of that oath to constitute a perjury, it is sound and eminently advisable to accept gladly as king the man whom London, the capital of the whole kingdom has received without objection,

125 and who moreover was a suitable candidate owing to his just claim of close relationship. Also we give warrant with confident expectation that if we accept the man and aid him with all our efforts he will be of very great service to the kingdom; because now that it is being plundered, torn to pieces, and trampled underfoot it is

130 acknowledged that it can be changed for the better, just at the very beginning of so great a calamity, by a man of resolution and soldierly qualities, who, exalted by the might of his vassals and by the fame of his wise brothers, will, supported by their assistance, bring to greater perfection whatever is thought to be lacking in him."

135 Therefore, swayed by these arguments . . . the archbishop, with the bishops and numerous clergy present, consecrated and annointed him as king over England and Normandy.

Gesta Stephani, ed. and trans. K. R. Potter (Oxford, Clarendon Press, 1976), pp 10–13

(e) From (London) the king went to Oxford, where he recorded and ratified the solemn promises which he had made to God and the

140 people, and to holy church, on the day of his coronation. They were these: – First, he vowed that he would never retain in his own hands the churches of deceased bishops, but forthwith consenting to a canonical election would invest those who were chosen. Secondly, that he would not lay hands on the woods either of clerks or laymen

145 as King Henry had done, who continually impleaded those who took venison in their own woods, or felled and diminished them to supply their own wants. This kind of pleading was carried to so execrable a length, that if the king's supervisors set eye from a distance on a moneyed man, they forthwith reported that there was

150 waste whether it was so or not, that the owner might have to redeem it, though the charge was groundless. Thirdly, the king promised that the Danegeld, that is two shillings for a hide of land, which his predecessors had received yearly should be given up forever. These were the principal things which, among others, he promised in the

155 presence of God; but he kept none of them.

Chronicle of Henry of Huntingdon, ed. T. Forester (London, Henry G. Bohn, 1853), pp 263–4

Questions

★ *a* Construct a family tree for Stephen.

b How and when had Stephen and other nobles bound themselves 'by allegiance to the Empress' (extract *b* line 37)?

c What suggestions are there in these extracts that the rule of Henry I had been unpopular?

d Why should the Londoners have been so keen to see Stephen installed as king?

e What arguments are put forward in extract *d* to explain why the oath to Matilda should be set aside? How convincing are these arguments?

f Make a list of the factors which the extracts suggest enabled Stephen to gain the throne. Is any single factor pre-eminently important?

g What practice is being referred to in lines 141–3 in extract *e*?

h What impressions can we gain about the support Stephen had at the time of his coronation from these extracts?

i Which of the extracts is most and least favourable to Stephen? Give reasons for your answer.

j What do the extracts suggest about the laws of succession to the throne at this time?

2   The fall of the bishops

(a) In 1139 . . . the poison of malice, long nurtured in King Stephen's mind, at length burst forth to be observed by all. Reports were being spread in England that Earl Robert might arrive from Normandy at any moment with his sister, and since, in expectation
5   of this, many were deserting the king in deed as well as thought he tried to make up for his losses by wrongs to many. A number too, on mere suspicion of siding against him he arrested in his own court, in a manner unbefitting a king, and forced them to surrender of their castles and any terms he liked. There were then in England two very
10   powerful bishops, Roger of Salisbury and his nephew through his brother, Alexander of Lincoln . . . Some powerful laymen, vexed that they would be surpassed by clerks in the amassing of wealth and the size of their castles, nourished within their hearts an unseen grudge of envy. And so they poured forth to the king the grievances
15   that had formed in their minds. The bishops, they said, forgetting they were churchmen, were mad with a rage for castle-building; no-one should doubt that all this was being done for the king's ruin, for the time when, immediately on the Empress's arrival, they could meet their lady and hand over the castles, influenced by the
20   recollection of her father's favours; therefore they must be anticipated with all speed and compelled to surrender their fortifications . . . The chief men kept on urging this. The king,

though easily swayed owing to his excessive favour towards them, pretended for some time not to listen to their cajolement of his ears,
25 softening their bitter accusations either through regard for religion where bishops were concerned or, as I think more probable, because he disliked exposing himself to censure. In the end he did not delay execution of what the great men had advised . . .

When a council of the leading men was held at Oxford about June
30 24th the aforesaid bishops arrived also. The Bishop of Salisbury was most unwilling to set out . . . Then, as if fortune were favouring the king's wishes, a brawl arose between the bishop's men and those of Alan Count of Brittany about claims on lodgings, with the lamentable result that the Bishop of Salisbury's men, who were
35 sitting at table, leapt up to fight before they had finished their meal. The contest was carried on first with abusive language, then with swords. Alan's followers were put to flight and his nephew almost killed, nor did the bishop's men gain their victory without loss of blood, since many were wounded and one knight slain. The king,
40 taking the opportunity, ordered the bishops to be summoned by the old fomentors or trouble to satisfy his court for their men's disturbance of its peace, the means of satisfaction to be surrender of the keys of their castles as guarantees of their trustworthiness. When they were ready to give satisfaction but hesitated about the surrender
45 of the castles he put them under close arrest to prevent their going away. Then he brought Bishop Roger, without charging him, and the chancellor . . . in chains, to Devizes, on the chance of obtaining the handing over of the castle . . . Devizes itself was surrendered after three days, when the bishop had imposed on himself a
50 voluntary fast, that by undergoing this suffering he might influence the mind of the Bishop of Ely, who had taken possession of the place.

William of Malmesbury, *Historia Novella*, trans. K. R. Potter (London, Nelson, 1955), pp 25–7

(b) (Roger of Salisbury) was reckoned next to the king in the whole government of the kingdom. So he, though he enjoyed the king's
55 strong affection, though he was given particular charge of all the business of court and kingdom, yet showed more affection and friendship in his sympathy for the children of King Henry. He promised, but in secret, to avoid offending the king, that he would most loyally keep faith with them and grant them zealous aid, and
60 his castles, which he had built elaborately, he was filling on a very lavish scale with weapons and supplies of food, shrewdly combining service to the king with waiting till the time should come when those others arrived in England and he could help them with the utmost vigour and speed . . . everywhere he went, and especially to the
65 king's court, he was encircled by a large and numerous bodyguard of troops, on pretence that he was leading them to help the king . . .

His nephews, too, who bore the titles of Bishop of Lincoln and
Bishop of Ely . . . agreed with this policy, and disregarding the holy
and simple manner of life that befit a Christian priest they devoted
70 themselves so utterly to warfare and the vanities of this world that
whenever they attended court by appointment they too aroused
general astonishment on account of the extraordinary concourse of
knights by which they were surrounded on every side. The Count of
Meulan, and those other adherents of the king who were on terms
75 of the closest intimacy with him, indignant at this splendid pomp of
the bishops, were inflamed against them with a furious blaze of
envy, and far from stifling the fire of their malice, once it was alight
they made many shameful and slanderous accusations of them to the
king. For they went on saying that those bishops owned the primacy
80 of the kingdom, all the splendour of their wealth, their whole force
of men for personal ostentation and profit, not for the king's honour;
that they had built castles of great renown, raised up towers and
buildings of great strength, and not to put the king in possession of
his kingdom, but to steal his royal majesty from him and plot against
85 the majesty of his crown; wherefore it would be judicious and was
most expedient for the king's peace to lay hands on them, that they
might give up to the king for his honour the castles and whatever else
could give rise to strife and wars, but that there should be yielded to
their disposal, in pious and Catholic fashion, what pertained to the
90 Church and to the sacred character and rights of a bishop. If the king,
they said, were minded to follow their advice as he relied on their
valour and wisdom, he would arrest those men without formalities
and put them in custody, not as bishops but as sinners against the
pacific office of a bishop and suspected enemies of his peace and
95 public order, until . . . the king was safe from suspicion of rebellion
(the charge alleged against the bishops) and his country was more
tranquil. On hearing these counsels, which they, goading him
perpetually, put before him with more envy and suspicion than piety
and justice, the king was in a quandary and great indecision of mind,
100 since on the one hand it was a serious and unlawful step to commit a
disrespectful assault on the priestly order, and on the other it went
against the grain and seemed a slight not to listen to his intimate
advisers and the chief men of his court. At length, overcome by their
persistent entreaties and the constant and vehement pressure that
105 they brought to bear, for his own honour and the peace of the
kingdom he allowed them to do to the bishops as they asked . . .
    So, when the bishops had assembled at court with the utmost
ostentation . . . a brawl suddenly arose between the bishops' knights
and the king's knights at the instigation of the crafty Count of
110 Meulan and some others. Those members of the king's party who
were present, especially those who appeared to be in the secret of the
aforesaid plot, took up arms, arrayed themselves in bands, and made
a headlong assault on the supporters of the bishops. When they had

captured some and killed others, and put a great many shamefully to
115 flight in all directions . . . they returned to the king as though they
had won a victory over their enemies, and when a general council of
the ill-disposed had been held, they hastened in a body to arrest the
bishops as if they were offenders against the king's majesty. And the
bishops, hearing of the shameful scattering of their men, were
120 preparing for flight . . . when . . . the king's followers, entering
their lodgings in arms and finding the Bishops of Salisbury and
Lincoln, brought them swiftly to the king . . . But the Bishop of Ely
. . . fled . . . to his uncle's castle at Devizes . . . The king coming to
Devizes brought with him the two bishops under close guard, and
125 gave orders that they should be lodged dishonourably apart from
each other and grievously tormented by insufficient diet and his chief
secretary, the son of the Bishop of Salisbury, who had already been
captured and put in chains, should be hanged on high right before the
castle entrance if the Bishop of Ely did not after all hand over the
130 castle and admit the king's forces . . . However, by advice of their
friends . . . they were persuaded to satisfy the king's wishes.

So the bishops, handing over to the king their castle and others
they had held, were going back soon afterwards, humble and
downcast and stripped of all their empty and ostentatious splendour,
135 to hold their church property in the simple fashion that befits a
churchman . . .

> *Gesta Stephani*, ed. and trans. K. R. Potter (Oxford,
> Clarendon Press, 1976), pp 72–9

(c) At the same time there was serious disorder in England. Roger,
bishop of Salisbury, a man of great wealth, who had powerful
friends and strong castles as befitted one who had enjoyed authority
140 over all England during the lifetime of King Henry, was the most
discredited of all the magnates in the kingdom because he was
suspected of betraying his king and lord, Stephen, and giving
support to the Angevin party. He was backed by his kinsmen and
accomplices, namely his son, who was the king's chancellor, and his
145 very powerful nephews, the bishops of Lincoln and Ely. These great
men, emboldened by the accumulation of immense wealth of all
kinds, rashly began to oppress the magnates round them in various
ways. Goaded by savage provocations, a number of men formed a
league against them and, seizing an opportune moment rose
150 simultaneously and attempted to repay them in their own coin for
the injuries inflicted. So the two brothers, Count Waleran and Earl
Robert, with Alan of Dinan and a number of others stirred up a
quarrel with the household of the bishops at Oxford, and after
several men on both sides had been killed took Roger and Alexander
155 prisoner. The bishop of Ely, however . . . hurried straight off to
take possession of the very powerful fortress of Devizes, occupied
the castle after devastating all the country round about with fire, and

resolved to hold it against the king with all the forces he could muster. On hearing this the king, in a rage, advanced his army
160 against the place and . . . vowed with many threats that Bishop Roger should be allowed no food until the hostile castle was handed over to him. He also captured the bishop's son, Roger le Poer, and commanded him to be hanged outside the gate in full view of the rebels. It happened that his mother, who was the bishop's
165 concubine, was defending the main castle. At length the bishop of Salisbury, with the king's permission, spoke to his nephew and heaped reproaches on him because, when he had seen trouble breaking out, he had not returned to his own diocese but had gone off in a rage to a place that was another's and, by recklessly scorching
170 the earth, had condemned many thousands to starvation. While the haughty nephew and his retainers obstinately persisted in their rebellion, and the angry king commanded that Roger le Poer should be hanged on a gallows immediately, the distressed mother . . . sent an envoy at once to the king and handed over the strong castle she
175 was holding as a ransom for his enemies. In this way the bishop of Ely was made powerless and he and his remaining supporters ruefully acquiesced in the surrender.

> The Ecclesiastical History of Orderic Vitalis, ed. Marjorie Chibnall (6 vols, Oxford, O.U.P., 1969–80), vol V, pp 530–5

(d) It happened the same year that Roger, bishop of Salisbury, Alexander, bishop of Lincoln, and Nigel, bishop of Ely, nephews of
180 the same Roger, met at the king's court; and a tumult having arisen, the servants of the bishops, among the rest of the mob, cut down a certain nephew of Alan, earl of Richmond, who afterwards died. In consequence of this, the same earl laid an accusation before the king against the bishops, that the disturbance was raised by their faction in
185 a plot against the king's safety. Bishop Nigel speedily escaped from the court by a clandestine flight to his fortresses; and the king felt all the more excited to revenge himself upon bishops Roger and Alexander, whom he compelled (by totally depriving them of food) to surrender their castles, with the abundant treasures which they
190 laid up in them.

> John of Hexham, History of the Church of Hexham in J. Stevenson, The Church Historians of England, vol IV, Part I (London, Seeleys, 1856), p 13

(e) After this (the Battle of the Standard, 1138 and the elevation of Theobald to the archdiocese of Canterbury), the king, residing at Oxford, became so depraved by evil counsel, that, through his greediness for money, he laid his impious hands on ecclesiastics,
195 and, paying no deference to holy orders, sullied his royal character with an indelible stain. Although but a short time before he had

received, with apparent kindness, Roger of Salisbury and Alexander of Lincoln, at that time the most noble and powerful bishops in England, yet on a sudden, as though they had been the vilest of
200 characters, and guilty of the most heinous crimes, he seized them, shut them up, and confined them with chains, as well as despoiled them of their property and castles.

. . . And when the illustrious king Henry exacted from all the prelates and nobles of the realm the oath to observe fidelity to his
205 daughter in the succession of the kingdom, the bishop of Salisbury not only readily took the oath himself, but like a prudent man and second to the king, carefully explained it, as the king required him to do, for the information of those who were about to swear. But on the death of Henry, who had been the author of all his temporal
210 grandeur, he was faithless towards his lawful heirs, in order that he might entice Stephen to join his party, who was bound in the same obligation; and thus not only was he fearless of committing perjury himself, but he gave a memorable example of it to others. On the advancement of Stephen to the throne, he conducted himself in such
215 a manner towards him, as to prove, by his devotion to his cause, the singular confidence which was reposed in him. Stephen was, however, ungrateful for these benefits, and was appointed God's avenger against this very bishop, whose deeds were never consistent with his dignity; and so did he distress him, as though he had been a
220 person of no importance, first by imprisonment, then by want of food, and lastly by the threat of inflicting punishment upon his nephew (who had been the king's chancellor), that he gave up the two noble castles, in which his treasures were deposited . . . At length, the aged bishop, worn down with grief and driven to
225 madness, was induced both to do and to say things utterly unbecoming, excited thereto by the loss of those things in the building up and accumulating of which he had so extremely offended God; and he concluded a most conspicuous life by a most lamentable death, through divine appointment. Alexander, bishop
230 of Lincoln, who had been made captive with him, was harassed by similar methods to resign the fortress he had built; and on relinquishing them he was released, though not without difficulty. These proceedings, however, did not produce favourable results to the king, though he had been the rod of God's fury against these
235 memorable bishops; for instigated either by personal hatred or anxiety after money, he paid very little deference to the sacred orders . . .

William of Newburgh, *Historia Rerum Anglicarum*, trans. in J. Stevenson, *The Church Historians of England*, vol IV, Part II (London, Seeleys, 1856), pp 412–3

Questions

a   According to the extracts, by what methods was Stephen trying to retain support before the arrest of the bishops?

b   What were the main reasons for lay hostility towards the bishops?

c   How do the extracts differ in their accounts of Stephen's reactions to the power of the bishops?

★ d   Who were the main opponents of the bishops?

e   In what ways do extracts *a*, *b* and *c* differ in their accounts of how the disputes at Oxford arose?

f   Compare the accounts of the ending of the siege of Devizes in extracts *a*, *b* and *c*.

g   Compare the attitudes of extracts *b*, *c* and *e* to Roger, bishop of Salisbury.

h   What do the extracts tell us about how some bishops behaved in this period?

i   Which extract is the most favourable to Stephen, and which the least? Justify your choice.

3   Matilda's failure in 1141

(a) At that time (Spring 1141) the greater part of England looked up to Matilda's authority with respect; her brother Robert, constantly with her, increased her prestige in every fitting way, by speaking affably to the chief men, making many promises, either intimidating
5 the opposition or urging it to peace by his envoys and beginning the restoration of justice and the ancestral laws and peace in every region that supported the Empress. It is well established that if the other members of his party had trusted his restraint and wisdom they would not afterwards have endured such a turn of ill-fortune. The
10 lord legate was also at hand to serve the Empress with what seemed to be a zealous loyalty. But . . . when it was thought she might at once gain possession of the whole of England, everything was changed. The Londoners, who had always been under suspicion and in a state of secret indignation, then gave vent to expressions of
15 unconcealed hatred; they even laid a plot, it is said, against their lady and her companions. The latter, forewarned of it and avoiding it, gradually left the city in good order with a kind of military discipline. The Empress was accompanied by the legate, David King of Scots, uncle of that woman of masculine spirit, her brother
20 Robert, then as always sharing his sister's fortunes in everything, and, to put it briefly, by all her adherents, unharmed to a man. The Londoners, learning of their departure dashed into their lodgings and carried off whatever had been left in haste.

William of Malmesbury, *Historia Novella*, trans. K. R. Potter (London, Nelson, 1955), pp 56–7

(b) The Empress having treated with the Londoners, lost no time in
25 entering the city with a great attendance of bishops and nobles: and
being received at Westminster with a magnificent procession, took
up her abode there for some days to set in order the affairs of the
kingdom. Her first care was to take measures for the good of God's
holy church, according to the advice of good men . . . The citizens
30 (of London) also prayed her that they might be permitted to live
under the laws of King Edward, which were excellent, instead of
under those of her father, King Henry, which were grievous. But
refusing to accept good advice, she very harshly rejected their
petition, and in consequence there was a great tumult in the city; and
35 a conspiracy being formed against her, the citizens, who had
received her with honour, now attempted to seize her person with
indignity. Being, however, forewarned by some of them, she fled
shamefully with her retinue, leaving all her own and their apparel
behind.

The Chronicle of Florence of Worcester, trans. T. Forester
(London, Henry G. Bohn, 1854), pp 281–2

40 (c) So when at last by receiving hostages and men's homage she had
brought the greater part of the kingdom under her sway, and on this
account, was mightily puffed up and exalted in spirit, finally she
came to London with a vast army at the request of the inhabitants,
who met her with entreaties. And when the citizens thought she had
45 attained to joyous days of peace and quietness and that the calamities
of the kingdom had taken a turn for the better, she sent for the richest
men and demanded from them a huge sum of money, not with
unassuming gentleness, but with a voice of authority. They
complained that they had lost their accustomed wealth owing to
50 the strife in the kingdom, that they had spent a great deal to relieve
the acute famine that threatened them, that they had always obeyed
the king until they were brought to the extremity of want, and
therefore they made humble and dutiful petition to her that she
might take pity on their misfortune and low estate, set a limit to the
55 exaction of money from them, spare the harassed citizens, even for a
little while, the burden of any extraordinary payment; later, when
after the lulling of the disturbances of war throughout the kingdom
peace returned with more security, they would aid her the more
eagerly in proportion as their wealth expanded. When the citizens
60 expressed themselves in this way she, with a grim look, her forehead
wrinkled into a frown, every trace of a woman's gentleness removed
from her face, blazed into unbearable fury, saying that many times
the people of London had made very large contributions to the king,
that they had lavished their wealth on strengthening him and
65 weakening her, that they had previously conspired with her enemies
for her hurt, and therefore it was not just to spare them in any respect
or make the smallest reduction in the money demanded. On hearing

this the citizens went away gloomily to their homes without gaining
what they asked.

Gesta Stephani, ed. and trans. K. R. Potter (Oxford, Clarendon Press, 1976), pp 120–3

70 (d) Just about this time too the queen, a woman of subtlety and a
man's resolution, sent envoys to the countess and made earnest
entreaty for her husband's release from his filthy dungeon . . . but
when she was abused in harsh and insulting language and both she
and those who had come to ask on her behalf completely failed to
75 gain their request, the queen, expecting to obtain by arms what she
could not by supplication, brought a magnificent body of troops
across in front of London from the other side of the river and gave
orders that they should rage most furiously around the city with
plunder and arson, violence and the sword, in sight of the countess
80 and her men. The people of London then were in grievous trouble.
On the one hand their land was being stripped before their eyes and
reduced by the enemy's ravages to a habitation for the hedgehog
(Isaiah 14:23), and there was no one ready to help them; on the other
that new lady of theirs was going beyond the bounds of moderation
85 and sorely oppressing them, nor did they hope that in time to come –
she would have mercy or compassion for them, seeing that at the
very beginning of her reign she had no pity on her subjects and
demanded what they could not bear. Therefore they judged it
worthy of consideration to make a new pact of peace and alliance
90 with the queen and join together with one mind to rescue their king
and lord from his chains . . .
    So when the countess, confident of gaining her will, was waiting
for the citizens' answer to her demand the whole city, with the bells
ringing everywhere as the signal for battle, flew to arms, and all,
95 with the common purpose of making a most savage attack on the
countess and her men, unbarred the gates and came out in a body,
like thronging swarms from beehives. She, with too much boldness
and confidence, was just bent on reclining at a well-cooked feast, but
on hearing the frightful noise from the city and getting secret
100 warning from someone about the betrayal on foot against her she
with all her retinue immediately sought safety in flight . . . their
flight had hardly taken them further than the suburbs when . . . a
mob of citizens . . . entered their abandoned lodgings and found and
plundered everywhere all that had been left behind in the speed of the
105 unpremeditated departure.

Gesta Stephani, ed. and trans. K. R. Potter (Oxford, Clarendon Press, 1976), pp 122–5

Questions

a Who is Matilda's 'brother Robert' (extract *a* line 2)?

b   Who is 'the lord legate' (extract *a* line 10)? Why is his support of Matilda so important?

★ *c*   Why should William of Malmesbury remark that the Londoners 'had always been under suspicion' (extract *a* line 13)?

d   Why did the Londoners want Matilda to moderate her demands of them?

e   Who is 'the queen' (extract *d* line 70)?

★ *f*   How had Matilda been able to take over the running of the kingdom?

g   What explanations does extract *d* add to the explanations of extracts *a–c* of why the Londoners wanted to be rid of Matilda?

h   How do the extracts differ in their accounts of how the Londoners went about getting Matilda out of London?

i   What impression do you gain of Matilda's character from these extracts?

j   What conclusions can you draw about how the authors of the extracts expected women to behave?

k   Which extract is most favourable to Matilda and which is least favourable? Justify your answer.

★ *l*   Compare Matilda's actions in 1141 with those of Stephen in 1135–6. What do they tell us about monarchical power in this period?

4   The end of the civil war

(a) So when the duke (Henry) . . . had gained a number of towns and a great many castles in these regions with energy and spirit, and had, by force of arms, already brought almost half England over to his side, he made rapidly for Wallingford which was being closely
5 besieged with two castles built in its neighbourhood, intending to give help to his men; and coming to Crowmarsh, a castle rising on a very high mound in front of Wallingford with only the river in between, he ordered his troops to attack it with great vigour on every side. When . . . the king's men, who on hearing of the duke's
10 arrival had withdrawn to places where they could not be seen, though a few kept up a show of resistance in the outer part of the castle, burst out in small parties from different hiding-places and made a gallant charge on those who had already climbed the mound and entered the outer part of the castle, and capturing some and
15 killing others they compelled by their valour the whole body to give way. Yet the duke was not broken by a disaster like this or in any degree reduced to despair; rather did he become more resolute the more often he received a blow from his opponents, and collecting a very large army from all his adherents he laid very close siege to the
20 castle. When the king learnt of this by report he hastily sent three hundred knights to Oxford, because it was near, ordering them to harass the duke's army with the help of the local barons; and so, with

both sides making daily raids on each other, the people of the country endured very many hazards. And at once the king, gathering an inexpressibly large army from every part of England, accompanied also by his son Eustace and many earls and countless barons, came to Wallingford; and as the two armies, in all their warlike array, stood close to each other, with only a river between them, it was terrible and very dreadful to see so many thousands of armed men eager to join battle with drawn swords, determined to the general prejudice of the kingdom, to kill their own relatives and kin.

Wherefore the leading men of each army, and those of deeper judgement were greatly grieved and shrank, on both sides, from a conflict that was not merely between fellow countrymen but meant the desolation of the whole kingdom, thinking it wise to raze to the ground the castle that was the seed-bed of war and then, making a truce between the two parties, to join all together for the establishment of peace. When this plan had at last been generally approved and adopted, after a private interview that the duke and the king had alone about making peace between them, they laid down their arms for the time being and went away individually to their own homes . . .

Then the king . . . still, on the advice of some barons who especially favoured war and strife, prepared to go on resisting the duke and attacking him. But at once he yielded to the advice of the Bishop of Winchester, who made himself a mediator between the duke and the king for the establishment of peace, and consented to the duke's inheriting England after his death provided he himself, as long as he lived, retained the majesty of the king's lofty position . . .

> *Gesta Stephani*, ed. and trans. K. R. Potter (Oxford, Clarendon Press, 1976), pp 236–41

(b) While this dispute between the king and the duke was protracted with doubtful issue, Eustace, the son of Stephen . . . died prematurely . . . affording, by his death, an admirable opportunity for laying the basis of a reconciliation between the princes . . . and their men, pacifically inclined, anxiously turned their thoughts to persuade and accomplish a reconciliation – for the father, being agonized beyond measure at the death of a son, his destined successor, relaxed in his warlike preparations, and listened with more than usual patience to the language of peace. The duke, too, regarding the counsels of the wise, who spoke upon the preference of an honourable and firm compact to dubious chances; a solemn and salutary conference was effected between them. By the mediation of their friends, piously and prudently proving for the public good, a peace was cautiously made, and firmly established between them. It was decreed, that, for the future, Stephen should reign solely in England, with the dignity and honour of a legitimate sovereign, and

that Henry should succeed him in the kingdom, as his lawful
heir . . .

> William of Newburgh, *Historia Rerum Anglicarum*, trans. in
> J. Stevenson, *The Church Historians of England*, vol IV, Part
> III (London, Seeleys, 1856), pp 440–1

(c) But the duke, under no alarm, though his forces were inferior to
70 the king's . . . marched in good order against the enemy. The royal
troops, when, unexpectedly, they perceived the duke's army drawn
up in battle array in their front, were struck with a sudden panic, but
the king, not disheartened, gave orders that his troops should march
from their camp prepared for battle. Then the traitorous nobles
75 interfered, and proposed among themselves terms of peace. They
loved, indeed, nothing better than discussion; but they had no
inclination for war, and felt no desire to exalt either the one or the
other of the pretenders to the crown, so that by humbling his rival
they themselves might become entirely subject to the other. They
80 preferred that, the two being in mutual fear, the royal authority
should, with respect to themselves, be kept in abeyance. The king
and the duke, therefore, being sensible of the treachery of their
adherents, were reluctantly compelled to make a truce between
themselves . . . and the king and the duke had a conference without
85 witnesses, across a rivulet, on the terms of a lasting accommodation
between themselves, during which the faithlessness of their nobles
was anxiously considered. At this meeting the business of the treaty
was only entered upon, its completion being deferred to another
opportunity.

> *Chronicle of Henry of Huntingdon*, trans. T. Forester (London,
> Henry G. Bohn, 1853), pp 292–3

Questions

★   *a*   When had Henry become duke of Normandy?
★   *b*   How had Henry's fortunes improved in 1152?
     c   What do lines 1–20 of extract *a* tell us about Henry's character?
     d   Why according to the author of extract *a* did the 'leading men of
         each army' want to make peace?
     e   What factors strengthened the likelihood of peace being made in
         1153 according to extract *b*?
     f   In what ways do the attitudes towards the nobles and their role in
         the bringing about of an accommodation between Stephen and
         Henry in extracts *a* and *c* differ?

5   The character of King Stephen

(a) So the king . . . was energetic in calming the kingdom and
establishing peace; he showed himself good-natured and agreeable

to all; he restored the disinherited to their own; in awarding ecclesiastical benefices he was completely immune from the sin of
5 simony; in dealing with cases and calling men to account he did nothing under the influence of presents or the sake of money; he bowed with humble reverence to all who were bound by any religious vows; he made himself affable and amenable to all of whatever age. He was even of such a kindly and gentle disposition
10 that he commonly forgot a king's exalted rank and in many affairs saw himself not superior to his men, but in every way their equal, sometimes actually their inferior.

Gesta Stephani, ed. and trans. K. R. Potter (Oxford, Clarendon Press, 1976), pp 22–3

(b) Overwhelmed, and with good cause, by the affliction of this disaster he appealed to his mother (Matilda), but she herself was in
15 want of money and powerless to relieve his great need. He also appealed to his uncle, the Earl of Gloucester, but he, brooding like a miser over his moneybags, preferred to meet his own requirements only. As all in whom he trusted were failing him in this critical moment he finally, it was reported, sent envoys in secret to the king
20 as a kinsman, and begged him in friendly and imploring terms to regard with pity the poverty that weighed upon him and hearken compassionately to one who was bound to him by close ties of relationship and well disposed to him as far as it depended on himself. On receiving this message the king, who was ever full of
25 pity and compassion, hearkened to the young man, and by sending money as had been asked he gladly helped one whom, as his rival for the kingship and utterly opposed to him, he should have deprived of any kind of aid. And though the king was blamed by some for acting not only unwisely, but even childishly, in giving money and so
30 much support to one to whom he should have been implacably hostile, I think that what he did was more profound and more prudent, because the more kindly and humanely a man behaves to an enemy the feebler he makes him and the more he weakens him.

Gesta Stephani, ed. and trans. K. R. Potter (Oxford, Clarendon Press, 1976), pp 206–7

(c) Let me be allowed not to hide the truth, with all respect for a very
35 kindly man, who, if he had acquired the kingdom in a lawful way and in administering it had not lent trusting ears to the whispers of the ill-disposed, would certainly have lacked little that adorns the royal character. The result was that under him the treasures of some churches were plundered and their landed property given to laymen;
40 churches belonging to clerks were sold to strangers; bishops were made prisoner and compelled to alienate their property; abbacies were granted to unfit persons either to oblige friends or to pay off debts. But I think these things should not be attributed to him so

much as to his conncellors, who used to urge upon him that he
45 should never lack money while the monasteries were full of treasure.
William of Malmesbury, *Historia Novella*, trans. K. R. Potter
(London, Nelson, 1955), p 20

(d) . . . For under king Stephen, the law was powerless of necessity,
because the king was powerless. Some persons did whatever seemed
right to themselves; many of opposite inclinations did what in their
own minds they knew to be wrong. Indeed, at first sight, it seemed
50 as if England were cut in twain, some favouring the king, and others
the empress; while neither king nor empress had power effectually to
curb their adherents; for neither of them was able to exercise
complete authority, or maintain rigid discipline over their party, but
by denying them nothing they respectively restrained them from
55 revolt. . . .
William of Newburgh, *Historia Rerum Anglicarum*, trans. in
J. Stevenson, *The Church Historians of England*, vol IV, Part II
(London, Seeleys, 1856), pp 428–9

(e) Stephen was a man distinguished for skill in arms, but in other
respects almost a fool, save that he was rather inclined to the side of
evil.
Walter Map, *De Nugis Curialium: Courtiers Trifles*, ed. and
trans. M. R. James, revised by C. N. L. Brooke and
R. A. B. Mynors (Oxford, Clarendon Press, 1983), p 475

Questions

a   What is 'simony' (extract *a* line 5)?
★   b   Extract *b* describes events in 1147. What was Henry trying to do
in that year?
c   What evidence is there in extract *c* to suggest the occupation of
the author?
d   What does extract *d* suggest about Stephen's authority over his
supporters?
e   Do extracts *a–d* support Walter Map's verdict on Stephen's
character (extract *e*)?
f   Construct your own character sketch of Stephen.

6   The Treaty of Winchester

(a) Stephen, king of England, to the archbishops, bishops, abbots,
earls, justiciars, sheriffs, barons, and to all his liegemen of England,
greeting.
    Know that I, King Stephen, have established Henry, duke of
5 Normandy, as my successor in the kingdom of England, and have

recognised him as my heir by hereditary right; and thus I have given
and confirmed to him and his heirs the kingdom of England.

The duke in return for this honour and gift and confirmation
which I have made to him, has done homage to me, and given me
10   surety by oath. He has sworn that he will be my liegeman, and that
he will guard my life and honour by every means in his power
according to the agreements made between us which are described in
this charter.

I have also given an oath of surety to the duke, that I will guard his
15   life and honour by every means in my power, and that I will
maintain him as my son and heir in all things, and that I will do all I
can to guard him against all men . . .

Charter of Stephen describing the conditions of the 'Treaty of
Winchester', in *English Historical Documents 1042–1189*, vol.
II, eds D. C. Douglas and G. W. Greenaway (London, Eyre
and Spottiswoode, 1953), pp 404–5

(b) Stephen, king of England, and Henry, duke of Normandy, his
kinsman, were reconciled upon the eighth of the Ides of November
20   (6 November) . . . upon these terms: – First of all, the king, in the
presence of his bishops and earls, and the rest of his nobility,
acknowledged that duke Henry had an hereditary right to the
kingdom of England; and the duke gave free permission to the king
to hold the realm during the whole of his lifetime, if he so pleased;
25   but upon this understanding, that the king, the bishops, and the rest
of the nobility, should make oath, that after the king's decease, the
duke (if he were the survivor) should obtain peaceful and unopposed
possession of the kingdom. An oath was also made, that the
possessions which had been unlawfully seized by intruders should be
30   restored to those their ancient and lawful owners, in whose hands
they had been in the time of the excellent king Henry; and that the
castles, which had sprung up to the enormous number of three
hundred and seventy-five since the death of that sovereign should be
levelled to the ground.

Chronicles of Robert de Monte, in J. Stevenson, *The Church
Historians of England*, vol IV, Part II (London, Seeleys, 1856),
p 735

Question

R. H. C. Davis has described the treaty between Henry and
Stephen as a formal admission that the barons did not hold their
lands by the pleasure of the king. What evidence is there in the
two versions of the treaty to support this view?

VIII   Normandy, Wales, Scotland and Ireland

Introduction

In any study of the Normans in Britain it is sometimes easy to forget that their concerns ranged not only through England, but also to Scotland, Wales and, to a lesser extent, Ireland. Even more important is it to recall that the Norman kings of England were also usually dukes of Normandy. The government and control of Normandy was, therefore, a central problem for the king of England. Between 1066 and the time when Stephen effectively lost control of Normandy in 1144 (although he still hoped to win the duchy back) England and Normandy were ruled by separate rulers for only fifteen years: and for much of these fifteen years the king or duke was trying to effect the union of the two lands. The problems of governing the two cross-Channel areas were met by the kings' decision to govern by movement. William I rejected the idea of governing either England or Normandy by a viceroyalty, as Cnut had tried to govern Denmark. Instead he and his successors attempted to divide their time between the lands. This process is best illustrated by Henry I between 1106 and 1135. He divided his time between Normandy and England in proportion of nearly 5:3, visiting England eight times. Only thirteen whole years were spent either in Normandy or England (nine in Normandy and four in England). This government by movement had very significant consequences, not least in the increasing sophistication of bureaucratic institutions such as the Exchequer and the Chancery. It is for this reason that this unit contains a section on the battle of Tinchebrai in 1106. The nature of the evidence leads us to concentrate on its military importance here, but its result should serve as a reminder of the cross-Channel concerns of the Anglo-Norman kings, and, of course, their subjects.

Wales, too, provided the Normans with substantial cause for concern. Despite the bold statement of *The Anglo-Saxon Chronicle* that Harold 'conquered' Wales in 1063, and of Gerald of Wales that Henry I had 'finally subjugated' the country, the Welsh were not so easily vanquished. The progress of the Norman conquest of Wales varied with the strengths of the Marcher lords, the fluctuating fortunes of the Welsh princes and, of course, the other preoccupations of the king of England. Gradually Wales was overcome, but the process lasted until the thirteenth century.

Norman relationships with Scotland also tended to fluctuate according to the relative strengths and weaknesses of the Scottish and Norman kings. Professor Barrow has remarked that William the Conqueror probably viewed the king of Scotland as not greatly different from the rest of the tribal kings in Wales and Ireland. Malcolm III (1058–93) made five attacks on England during his reign. After his marriage to Margaret, the sister of Edgar Aetheling, in c. 1070, he could have emerged as the focus of opposition to the Normans in Britain, but he was never able to achieve this, and William I and William Rufus were usually able to maintain some sort of nominal overlordship over the Scottish kings. Some of the Scottish kings between Malcolm III and David I welcomed this because it strengthened them in their struggles against their Norwegian rivals and the more troublesome Scottish mormaers. Under David I (1124–53) the power of the Scottish king increased considerably. David was able to cooperate with the traditional Scottish nobility and to strengthen his government by importing Norman ideas which he had seen at work during his upbringing at the court of Henry I. He tried to take advantage of Stephen's troubles by establishing Scottish rule over England north of the Tees and the Duddon, but Henry II was eventually able to assert Angevin authority there.

Ireland, according to Professor Barlow 'barely tempted Norman cupidity', and there was no political pressure put on Ireland by the rulers of England until Henry II's reign. However, the church in England came into contact with the Irish church, and Lanfranc, in particular, has been harshly criticised for his imperialistic intentions towards Ireland. Norman treatment of the national churches was usually 'imperialistic' but in Ireland's case there seemed little chance of Lanfranc, or Anselm, being able to translate any grandiloquent claim they might have had into reality. Indeed the relationship between the Normans and the Irish probably owed more to the internal politics of each country than any strong desire to gain control or accept overlordship. It suited Lanfranc to be seen as the primate of the Irish churches in his efforts to establish Canterbury's primacy over York, and links with Canterbury bolstered the authority of Irish bishops and kings within Ireland.

Further Reading

The outstanding work on the cross-Channel Norman Empire is J. Le Patourel, *The Norman Empire* (Oxford, O.U.P., 1976). G. W. S. Barrow, *Feudal Britain, 1066–1314* (paperback edn, London, 1971) is the best introduction to Wales and Scotland. D. Walker, *The Norman Conquerors* (Swansea, Christopher Davies, 1977) and A. C. Reeves, *The Marcher Lords* (Swansea, Christopher

Davies, 1983) are very useful on Wales, as G. W. S. Barrow, *Kingship and Unity: Scotland 1000–1316* (London, Edward Arnold, 1981) is invaluable for Scotland. For Lanfranc and Ireland, F. Barlow, *The English Church, 1066–1154* (London, Longman, 1979) is a helpful starting-point. J. A. Watt, *The Church and the Two Nations in Medieval Ireland* (Cambridge, C.U.P., 1970), although concentrating on the thirteenth century, has much of interest on Lanfranc and the Irish Church.

1 The Battle of Tinchebrai, 1106

(a) Upon the king's laying siege to the castle of Tinchebrai, the Duke of Normandy, having with him Robert de Bellême and the Earl of Morton with all their adherents, advanced against him. The king, on his side was not unprepared; for there were with him almost
5 all the chief men of Normandy, and the flower of the forces of England, Anjou and Brittany. The shrill trumpets sounded, and the duke, with his few followers boldly charged the king's numerous troops, and, well trained in the war of Jerusalem, his terrible onset repulsed the royal army. William, earl of Morton, also attacking it
10 from point to point, threw it into confusion. The king and the duke, with great part of their troops, fought on foot, that they might make a determined stand; but the Breton knights bore down on the flank of the duke's force, which, unable to sustain the shock, was presently routed. Robert de Bellême, perceiving this, saved himself by flight;
15 but Robert, duke of Normandy, and William, earl of Morton, were made prisoners . . .
> *The Chronicle of Henry of Huntingdon*, trans. and ed. T. Forester (London, Henry G. Bohn, 1853), p 242

(b) To his lord the priest of Sécz, the priest of Fécamp, sends greetings and prayers. I bring you good news, my lord, inasmuch as I realise you are eager for tidings in this matter. Our lord king fought
20 with his brother at Tinchebrai on 28 September at the third hour. Thus was the battle disposed. In the first line were the men of the Bessin, the Avranchin and the Contentin, and these were all on foot. In the second line was the king with his very numerous barons and these likewise were on foot. Seven hundred mounted knights were
25 placed with each line; and besides these the count of Maine, and Alan Fergaunt, count of Brittany, flanked the army with about a thousand mounted knights. All the camp followers and servants were removed far to the rear of the battle. The whole army of the king may be reckoned as having consisted of about forty thousand
30 men. When the battle had lasted only an hour, Robert of Bellême turned and fled, and all his men were dispersed. The count himself was captured, and the count of Mortain with his barons, and my friend, Robert of Estouteville. The rest all disappeared in flight. Wherefore the land became subject to the king. Nor must I fail to tell

35 you about this marvel: that the king in the battle lost only two men; and one was wounded, namely Robert de Bomrebosc. When I came to the king, he received me very graciously at Caen, and he willingly granted all those things which he had exacted from our land. And now, thank God, peace is restored in the land. Let us pray that it may
40 continue . . .

> Description of the battle of Tinchebrai given by a priest of Fécamp, in *English Historical Documents II 1042–1189* (London, Eyre and Spottiswoode, 1953), p 304

(c) As Henry besieged Tinchebrai, William earl of Morton, claimed the aid of the duke, and of Robert de Bellême and his other friends, and speedily obtained succour against the king . . . The king, however, persisted in carrying on the siege, and accepted the duke's
45 hostility, though it was worse than a civil war, in order to secure peace for the future . . . The Duke could not muster so many knights as his brother, but his army contained a more numerous body of infantry. In the opposite forces now in presence, brothers and kinsmen were arrayed on different sides, and some of them were
50 ready to exchange blows with each other . . . Several men of religion interfered to prevent so horrible a conflict, dreading to be the witnesses of the brothers shedding each other's blood . . . But after an attempt at mediation, the royal ambassadors announced on their return that the duke and his adherents preferred war at all hazards
55 rather than peace . . .

Henry assembled the commanders of his forces and laying before them his plan of operations in the battle, briefly directed them to act as time and circumstances required . . . He then drew out his troops in battle array, and they marched forward in well disciplined order.
60 Ranulf of Bayeux commanded the first division, Robert earl of Morton, the second, and William de Warenne the third . . . The king reserved the English and Norman infantry for his own command . . .

In the enemy's army William of Morton led the first division, and
65 Robert of Bellême commanded the rear. When the ranks met, . . . the troops were crowded so closely, and their weapons so locked together that it was out of their power to injure each other, and both parties in turn attempted in vain to break the impenetrable phalanx. Cries and shouts being raised from both armies, Elias made a rapid
70 charge with his auxiliaries on the flank of the duke's ill-armed infantry, in which two hundred and twenty-five of them presently fell. As soon as Robert of Bellême perceived this, he took flight, leaving the conquerors to deal with the duke's army, which was now in complete confusion.
75 One of Henry's chaplains seized the duke and delivered him to the king's guards.

> Adapted from Orderic Vitalis, *Ecclesiastical History of England*

and Normandy, vol IV, trans. T. Forester (London, Seeleys, 1854), pp 376–80

Questions

a Use the three extracts to try to establish how the forces of the king and the duke were drawn up on the battlefield and give an account of the battle.

b What differences do the extracts contain in their considerations of the numbers of the two armies?

c Compare the importance of cavalry and infantry in the battle.

d Which passage do you think was written soonest after the battle, and why?

★ e What happened to Robert, duke of Normandy, after the battle?

★ f Why did Anglo-Norman rebellions usually occur when the king of England was not duke of Normandy?

2 Wales

(a) While the English everywhere were being shaken by these storms (in 1087–8), and the inhabitants of the kingdom were fighting and slaying each other daily, as some tried to overthrow the king and others fought with determination in his support, the Welsh

5 king Gruffydd invaded England with his army, burning and slaying mercilessly around Rhuddlan. He seized much booty and led away some captives. So when Robert, the commander of Rhuddlan, returned home from the siege of Rochester and heard reports so terrible and damaging to him his heart was pierced with sorrow, and

10 he openly showed his fury by his dreadful threats . . .

Earlier Robert had been made commander of Hugh of Avranches' forces in the county of Chester. At that time the neighbouring Britons who are commonly called Gaels or Welsh were making savage attacks on King William and all his followers. So by the

15 king's command a castle was built at Rhuddlan to contain the Welsh, and was given to Robert with the duty of defending the kingdom of England against these barbarians. The warlike marcher lord often fought against this unruly people and slew many in battle after battle. After driving back the native Britons in fierce combat he

20 enlarged his territories and built a strongly fortified castle on the hill of Deganwy . . . For fifteen years he harried the Welsh mercilessly, invaded the lands of men who when they still enjoyed their original liberty had owed nothing to the Normans, pursued them through woods and marshes and over steep mountains and found different

25 ways of securing their submission. Some he slaughtered mercilessly on the spot like cattle; others he kept for years in fetters, or forced into a harsh and unlawful slavery. It is not right that Christians should so oppress their brothers, who have been reborn in the faith of Christ by holy baptism.

30 Pride and greed, which have a hold on the hearts of men
everywhere, were the incentives that drove the marcher lord,
Robert, to unrestrained plunder and slaughter . . . It happened that
on 3 July (prob. 1093) the Welsh king Gruffydd landed with three
ships on the shore under the rocky height called the Great Orme, and
35 the army of pirates scattered at once to prey on the coastal region like
ravening wolves . . . Meanwhile the cries of the crowd roused
Robert from a midday sleep, and made him aware of the hostile raid
on his land . . . He himself, all unprepared, pursued the Welsh with a
few men-at-arms . . . he ordered the few men with him, all
40 unprepared as they were, to fall on the Welsh while they were
stranded on the beach before the tide came in. They protested that
they were too few and the way down from the summit too steep.
Robert . . . flung himself down the difficult slope without his
hauberk . . . When they saw him with only a shield for protection,
45 accompanied by only a single knight, with one accord they flung
their javelins at this valiant lord, bore down his shield with the
weight of his missiles, and fatally wounded him . . . At last, he fell to
his knees . . . and all rushed upon him and, in full sight of his men,
cut off his head and fixed it on the mast of a ship as a sign of
50 victory . . .

   Adapted from *The Ecclesiastical History of Orderic Vitalis*, vol
   IV, ed. and trans. Marjorie Chibnall (Oxford, O.U.P.,
   1973), pp 134–41

(b) When William Longsword, King of England, heard of the
prowess of Gruffydd and his ferocity and his cruelty against the
French, he could not endure it, and roused the whole kingdom
against him, and came to Gwynedd with an abundance of troops of
55 horsemen and footmen, intending to abolish and destroy utterly all
of the people until there should be alive not so much as a dog. He had
purposed also to cut down all the woods and groves so that there
might not be shelter nor defence for the men of Gwynedd
henceforth. Thereupon he encamped and pitched his tents first in
60 Mur Castell, certain of the Welsh being his guides. When Gruffydd
heard this he assembled the host of the whole kingdom and went
against him to create obstacles for him in narrow places when he
descended from the mountains. And he (Rufus) was afraid and led
his hosts through the Perveddwlad until he reached Chester without
65 doing any kind of injury on that journey to the inhabitants of the
country. He did not take with him any kind of profit or gain except
one cow. He lost a great part of the knights and esquires and servants
and horses and many other possessions. Thus Gruffydd reduced the
French to nought.
70   Meanwhile, at all times, Gruffydd, and his host with him were
now before, now behind, now on the right, now on the left of them,
preventing them from doing any injury to his kingdom. If
Gruffydd had allowed his men to come to close quarters with them

in the woods, that would have been the last day for the King of
75 England and his Frenchmen.

The History of Gruffydd ap Cynan, ed. and trans. A. Jones
(Manchester, U.M.P., 1910), pp 140–3

(c) When war came and the Normans conquered England, this
land (Wales) they also added to their dominion and fortified with
numberless castles; they perseveringly civilized it after they had
vigorously subdued its inhabitants; to encourage peace they imposed
80 law and statutes on them; and they made the land so productive and
abounding in all kinds of resources that you would have reckoned it
in no wise inferior to the most fertile part of Britain. But when King
Henry died and the peace and harmony of the kingdom were buried
with him, the Welsh, who always cherished a deadly hatred of their
85 masters, broke their compact with them utterly, and appearing in
bands at different places, they made hostile raids in various
directions; they cleared the villages by plunder, fire, and sword,
burnt the houses, slaughtered the men. And first they advanced into
a district by the coast, called Gower, very pleasant and rich in every
90 kind of produce, and when the knights and footmen of the number
516 massed in one body against them they surrounded them on
every side and laid them all low with the edge of the sword. Then,
rejoicing greatly at this first success in their insurrection, they
streamed boldly over every quarter of Wales; addicted to every
95 crime, ready for anything unlawful, they spared no age, showed no
respect for any order, were not restrained from wickedness either by
time or place. When the first stirrings of this rebellion were reported
to the ears of the king, purposing to check their wanton recklessness
he sent to subdue them knights and archers whom he had hired at
100 very great expense. But some, when they had done many noble
deeds were killed there and others, unable to withstand the furious
assault of the enemy, after many toils and much waste of treasure
came back without honour . . . Therefore, when the Welsh were
troubling the land in this fashion, it seemed to the king that he was
105 striving in vain, in vain pouring out vast treasure to reduce them to
peace; and so, advised by more judicious counsel, he preferred to
endure their insolent rebellion for a time, in order that, with fighting
at a stand-still and disagreement setting them at variance, they might
either suffer a famine or turn on each other and be exterminated in
110 mutual slaughter. And indeed we have seen this happen in a short
while . . . These things, which happened in Wales at different times,
I have brought together and dealt with briefly, that I might not have
to stray from the course of my narrative . . .

Gesta Stephani, ed. and trans. K. R. Potter (Oxford,
Clarendon Press, 1976), pp 14–21

Questions

★ *a* To what events do lines 1–4 of extract *a* refer?
  b What is Orderic's attitude to Robert of Rhuddlan?
  c Compare the attitudes of the writers of extracts *a* and *b* to Gruffydd.
  d What do the extracts tell us about the process of the Norman conquest of Wales?
  e Extracts *a* and *b* are concerned with eleventh-century Wales: extract *c* is concerned with twelfth-century Wales. To what extent have Anglo-Welsh relationships changed between the 1090s and the mid-twelfth century?
  f Compare the attitudes of the writers of extracts *a* and *c* to the Welsh.

3 Scotland

(a) 1072 In this year king William led naval and land levies against Scotland and blockaded that country to seaward with his ships. He invaded the country with his land levies at the Forth, but gained no advantage from it. King Malcolm came and made his peace with
5 king William, gave hostages and became his vassal, and the king returned home with all his levies.

> Peterborough version (E) of *The Anglo-Saxon Chronicle*, trans. G. N. Garmonsway (London, Dent, 1953), p 208

(b) (1091) Whilst king William was out of England, king Malcolm invaded England from Scotland and harried a great part of it, until the good men who were governing this country sent levies against
10 him and turned him back. When king William in Normandy heard of this, he made ready for his departure and came to England, his brother, the duke Robert accompanying him. The king straightway had his levies called out, both the fleet and the land levies; but before he could reach Scotland, four days before Michaelmas, almost the
15 entire fleet was disastrously lost. The king and his brother marched with the land levies, but when king Malcolm heard that levies were approaching, he left Scotland and went into Lothian in England with his levies and there waited. Then when king William approached with his levies, duke Robert and prince Edgar intervened, and
20 succeeded in making peace between those kings, with the result that king Malcolm came to our king and became his man, rendering obedience to him in all respects as to his father before him, and confirmed it with oath. King William promised him, in land and in all things, all that he had formerly held under his father.
25   In this peace also prince Edgar was reconciled with the king. Then the kings parted in great friendship, but it was not to last long.

> Peterborough version (E) of *The Anglo-Saxon Chronicle*, trans. G. N. Garmonsway (London, Dent, 1953), pp 226–7

(c) (1093) . . . the king of Scotland sent and desired the fulfilment of the treaty which had been promised him: and king William summoned him to Gloucester, and sent hostages to him in Scotland,
30 followed by prince Edgar, and then afterwards men to meet him who brought him to the king with great ceremony. When, however, he came to the king he was not considered worthy of an audience of our king, nor of the assurances which had formerly been promised him. Hence they parted in great enmity, and king Malcolm went back
35 to Scotland. But quickly, after his arrival, he gathered together his levies, and invaded England, harrying with greater recklessness than was at all proper for him, when Robert, the earl of the Northumbrians with his men surprised and slew him. Morel of Bamburgh, who was the earl's steward and had spiritual affinity to
40 king Malcolm struck him down. With him was also slain his son Edward, who should have been king after him had he survived. When the good queen Margaret heard that her dearest lord and son had been thus betrayed, she became fatally distressed in mind and went to church with her priests. She received her last offices and
45 prayed to God that she might yield up her spirit. The Scots elected Donald, brother of Malcolm, king, and drove out all the English who had been with king Malcolm. Then when Duncan, king Malcolm's son, heard all that had taken place – he was in king William's court since his father had given him as a hostage to the
50 father of our king and he had remained so ever since – he came to the king and gave such pledges as the king demanded from him, and, with his consent, went to Scotland. With such English and French assistance as he could obtain, he deprived Donald, his kinsman, of the kingdom, and was received as king. But some of the Scots,
55 afterwards came together, and slew almost all his followers, and he himself with a few escaped. Thereafter they became reconciled, on condition that he never again introduced Englishmen or Frenchmen into that country.

Peterborough version (E) of *The Anglo-Saxon Chronicle*, trans. G. N. Garmonsway (London, Dent, 1953), pp 227–8

Questions

★ a What provoked William the Conqueror into leading his expeditionary force into Scotland in 1072?

★ b Who was the Prince Edgar mentioned in extract *b* (line 19)?

 c To what extent do the extracts suggest that the English kings consistently exercised authority over the Scottish king?

★ d What laws of succession to the Scottish throne does extract *c* suggest were in operation at this time? Was the method by which Donald attained the throne unusual in eleventh and twelfth-century Scotland?

★ e   What was the significance of Queen Margaret in late eleventh-
      century Scotland?

(d) (1136) At length a conference was held (at Durham) and a treaty
60 being concluded between the two kings, Henry, son of David, king
    of Scotland, did homage to king Stephen at York. With his father's
    earldom of Huntingdon the king gave him Carlisle and Doncaster,
    with all their appurtenances; and according to the account of some,
    who state that they were present at that convention, he promised
65 him that if he purposed to bestow upon any one the earldom of
    Northumberland, he would first cause the claim which Henry, son
    of the king of Scotland, might have upon it, to be fairly adjudicated
    in his court. King David restored to Stephen, king of England, four
    of the castles he had seized (Wark, Alnwick, Norham and
70 Newcastle); for the fifth, namely, Carlisle, had been ceded to him, an
    agreement with pledges being concluded by the subjects on each
    side.
          Richard of Hexham, *The Acts of King Stephen, and the Battle of
          the Standard*, trans. in J. Stevenson, *The Church Historians of
          England*, vol IV, Part I (London, Seeleys, 1856), p 39

(e) 1138. In this year David, king of Scotland, invaded this country
    with immense levies, determined to conquer it. He was met by
75 William, earl of Aumale, to whom the king had entrusted York, and
    by the other trustworthy men with a few followers; they fought
    against them, and put the king to flight at the battle of the Standard,
    and slew a great number of his host.
          Peterborough version (E) of *The Anglo-Saxon Chronicle*,
          trans. G. N. Garmonsway (London, Dent, 1953), p 226

(f) (1139) . . . peace was concluded between the two kings, by
80 means of envoys on these terms: Stephen, king of England, granted
    to Henry, son of David, king of Scotland, the earldom of
    Northumberland, except two towns, Newcastle and Bamburgh,
    with all the lands which he held before. But for these towns he was
    bound to give him towns of the same value in the south of England.
85 He directed also that the barons who held of the earldom, as many as
    chose, might make acknowledgement of their lands to earl Henry,
    and do homage to him, saving the fealty which they had vowed to
    himself; and this the most of them did. The king of Scotland and his
    son Henry, with all their descendants, were bound henceforward to
90 remain for the life amicable and faithful to Stephen, king of England.
    And to render their fidelity more secure they were pledged to give
    him as hostages five earls of Scotland . . . They were also bound to
    observe unalterably the laws, customs, and statutes which his uncle

king Henry had established in the county of Northumberland.
Richard of Hexham, *The Acts of King Stephen, and the Battle of the Standard*, trans. in J. Stevenson, *The Church Historians of England*, vol IV, Part I (London, Seeleys, 1856), p 58

Questions

★   *a*   Why was a treaty necessary between Stephen and David in 1136?
    b   Make a list of the terms of the treaties of 1136 and 1139.
    c   To what extent were the Scots worse off by the treaty of 1139?
    d   Account for the changes and continuity between the treaties of 1136 and 1139.

4   Canterbury and Ireland

(a) Whoever rules over others must not think it beneath him if he himself is subordinate to others; but rather let him humbly show to those who are appointed over him, in all things and for the love of God, that obedience which he wishes to receive from his own
5 subjects. Wherefore, I, Patrick, who have been chosen to rule Dublin, the capital city of Ireland, do hand to thee, my reverend father Lanfranc, primate of Britain and archbishop of the holy church of Canterbury, this charter of my profession; and I promise that I shall obey thee and thy successors in all things which pertain to
10 the Christian religion.

The oath of Patrick, bishop of Dublin, to Lanfranc, 1074.
Printed in J. A. Watt, *The Church and the Two Nations in Medieval Ireland* (Cambridge, C.U.P., 1970), p 217

(b) Lanfranc, archbishop not by his own merits but by the grace of God, sends Guthric, the glorious king of Ireland, his prayerful greetings. Dearest son, we received with honour our venerable brother and fellow bishop Patrick, whom your excellency sent to us
15 to be consecrated; with the grace of the Holy Ghost to help us we consecrated him in due form to his appointed duties; after his consecration we sent him back to his own see with our letter of commendation, as was the custom of our predecessors. Now although he brought us many good reports of you, glorious king,
20 matters worthy of much commendation, even so we think that it may be useful to encourage you in your laudable endeavours with some words of advice . . . There are said to be men in your kingdom who take wives from either of their own kindred or that of their deceased wives; others who by their own will and authority abandon
25 wives who are legally married to them; some who give their own wives to others and by an abominable exchange receive the wives of other men instead. For the sake of God and your own soul command that these offences and any other like them be corrected throughout

the land which you rule, and with God's help so treat your subjects
30 that those who love good may cherish it the more and those who lust
after evil may never venture to do wrong . . . I would have written
you a longer and more detailed letter, but that you have with you the
bishop whom we spoke of above.

> Lanfranc to Guthric, king of Dublin, 29 Aug. 1073–autumn
> 1074. Printed in *The Letters of Lanfranc, Archbishop of
> Canterbury*, eds and trans. H. Clover and M. Gibson
> (Oxford, Clarendon Press, 1979) pp 66–9

(c) Lanfranc, unworthy archbishop of the holy church of
35 Canterbury sends greetings and his blessing to the reverend
Domnall, bishop of Ireland, and to those who sent him the letter.

We were on a journey and far removed from the city in which we
have our episcopal see when we received the letter that your
messenger brought. Although we asked him to stay with us for at
40 least a few days, so that when we had fully studied the literature he
could take back the answer to your inquiries of which we were
capable, he refused to accede to our request, asserting very volubly
that he could not delay any longer. So we warn you, dearest
brethren, whom we love as a father, that the reply is inadequate
45 which we are giving you so briefly on so serious a matter.

You may be assured that it is absolutely beyond question that
neither the continental churches nor we English hold the view that
you think we hold concerning infants. We do all universally believe
that it is of great benefit to people of all ages to fortify themselves by
50 receiving the body and blood of the Lord during their lives and when
they are dying. But should it happen that baptized infants leave this
world at once, before they receive the body and blood of Christ, we
do not in any sense believe – God forbid! – that on this account they
are lost for eternity . . . Many of the holy martyrs racked by various
55 tortures departed from the body without being even baptized. Yet
the Church reckons them in the number of martyrs and believes
them to be saved . . . Let every believer who can understand that it is
a divine mystery eat and drink the flesh and blood of Christ not only
with his physical mouth but also with a tender and loving heart: that
60 is to say, with love and in the purity of a good conscience rejoicing
that Christ took on flesh for our salvation, hung on the cross, rose
and ascended; and following Christ's example and sharing in his
suffering so far as human weakness can bear it and divine grace
deigns to allow him. This is what it means to eat the flesh of Christ
65 and drink his blood truly and unto salvation . . .

You also sent problems of profane learning for us to elucidate; but
it does not befit a bishop's manner of life to be concerned with
studies of that kind. Long ago in our youth we did devote our time to

these matters, but when we came to pastoral responsibility we
70 decided to give them up altogether.

Lanfranc to Domnall Ua h-Énna, bishop of Munster, and his
colleagues 29 Aug. 1080–28 Aug. 1081. Printed in *The Letters
of Lanfranc Archbishop of Canterbury*, eds and trans. H. Clover
and M. Gibson (Oxford, Clarendon Press, 1979), pp 154–61

Questions

a   What does extract *a* suggest was the relationship between the
    Irish Church and the English Church?
b   What problems of the Irish Church are revealed by the extracts?
c   What theological problems does extract *c* consider?
d   What might the significance be of Lanfranc's use of the phrase
    'we English' in extract *c* line 47?
e   In what ways could these extracts bolster Lanfranc's authority in
    England?

Note on the Chronicle Sources

The *Anglo-Saxon Chronicle* is the most important English historical source prior to 1066. It was begun in King Alfred's reign and continued in a number of monastic houses recording events almost contemporaneously for about 250 years. There are three principal manuscript copies – the Abingdon (C), Worcester (D) and Peterborough (E) Chronicles. While these versions are probably derived from a common source there are important differences both of fact, interpretation and emphasis on local affairs. For example the Peterborough Chronicle is Godwinist in emphasis while the Worcester Chronicle is politically impartial, but pays special attention to Welsh and Scandinavian events. The Peterborough Chronicle is the only one to continue after 1100.

Guy of Amiens' authorship of the *Carmen de Hastingae Proelio* is a matter of some doubt although it is still accepted by a number of respected historians. If the bishop of Amiens, uncle of Guy, count of Ponthieu, was indeed the author then the poem was written before 1070 and was used by William of Poitiers.

HUGH THE CHANTOR became a canon of York c. 1100. By 1133 he was precentor and archdeacon and died in c. 1139. It appears that his *History of the Church of York* was completed in 1127 and the main theme of this work is the contest for the primacy of Britain between the sees of Canterbury and York.

EADMER was an Englishman born in c. 1064. From early in his life he was brought up at the monastery of Christ Church, Canterbury. From 1093 he became the constant companion of Anselm. Eadmer died in c. 1144. He wrote two major works, *Vita Sancti Anselmi* (The Life of St. Anselm) and *Historia Novorum* (A History of Recent Events). Both were largely completed by 1125. Eadmer's main purpose in his work was to describe the life of Anselm who became archbishop of Canterbury in 1093. Eadmer hated William Rufus because he treated Anselm so badly. He also deplored the Norman Conquest.

GEOFFREI GAIMAR wrote a history of England in verse. He probably composed his work in the early part of Stephen's reign. We know little of Gaimar's origins. He wrote for a patroness called Constance who came from a Lincolnshire family. He seems to have begun his work in Hampshire and subsequently moved north with his patroness. Gaimar appears to have been well connected at court, and his history contains a favourable view of William Rufus. Gaimar wrote in Norman–French.

The identity of the author of the *Gesta Stephani* is not known. R. H. C.

Davis has suggested that the work was written by Robert of Lewes, bishop of Bath. It is certainly well informed on events in the West Country. The work appears to be fairly contemporaneous, although it seems to have been written in two sections. The first, which favours Stephen and covers the years 1135–47 was probably written around 1148. The second, which favours Henry II, was composed in 1153.

The History of Gruffydd ap Cynan was probably written in the lifetime of his son Owain Gwynedd (1137–71). It was probably written in Latin first before being translated into Welsh. It contains no dates, but its detail can be substantiated by comparison with other sources. It is notably pro-Welsh.

RICHARD OF HEXHAM was a canon at Hexham where he became prior in 1141 until sometime between 1155 and 1167. His chronicle, *The Acts of King Stephen and the Battle of the Standard*, covers the years 1135–39. It was written fairly shortly after the events it describes and includes much information about affairs in the north of England which cannot be obtained elsewhere.

HENRY OF HUNTINGDON was born in Cambridgeshire or Huntingdonshire. He began writing in c. 1133 and wrote to c. 1154. He lived for a long time in the household of Alexander of Blois, bishop of Lincoln (1123–48). His *Historia Anglorum* was very popular and was probably written fairly contemporaneously once it reached Stephen's reign.

WILLIAM OF JUMIEGES was a Norman monastic historian writing around 1070. His chronicle, *Gesta Normannorum Ducum*, was originally dedicated to William the Conqueror. While William of Jumièges is undoubtedly a panegyrist intent on praising the Conqueror and justifying his claims to the English throne, he is nevertheless the most objective and fair-minded of the contemporary Norman historians.

WILLIAM OF MALMESBURY was a monk at the abbey of Malmesbury in Wiltshire. He was born in c. 1095 and died in 1143. He wrote *De Gestis Regum Anglorum* in 1125. His *Historia Novella*, dedicated to Matilda's half-brother, Robert, earl of Gloucester, was composed more or less contemporaneously in Stephen's reign. William usually based his writing on a careful examination of the evidence available to him and he tried to be fair in his work on Stephen and Roger, bishop of Salisbury, but he had a strong prejudice against any great man who offended the monastic order. Like many chroniclers, William wrote both to instruct and to entertain his readers.

WALTER MAP was not a historian but a court satirist, noted for his realistic character sketches. He wrote the *De Nugis Curialium* between 1181 and 1193. He was well-travelled and a member of Henry II's household for many years. His work was heavily influenced by his knowledge of classical literature. Born in c. 1140, he died in c. 1208/10.

ROBERT DE MONTE (or DE TORIGNI) was a monk of Bec from 1128 and abbot of Mont-Saint-Michel from 1154. He was a well-travelled and well-connected man. He wrote from 1139 and from 1147 his chronicle (of the creation to 1186) is fairly contemporaneous.

WILLIAM OF NEWBURGH is widely regarded as an outstanding historian. His *Historia Rerum Anglicarum* was based on a number of diverse sources, which William used critically. The work was begun in c. 1196 and completed in 1198, and is a vital source for the reign of Henry II.

WILLIAM OF POITIERS, archdeacon of Lisieux, wrote his admiring account of the Conqueror, *Gesta Willelmi ducis Normannorum et regis Anglorum*, around 1071. He had previously served the duke both as a soldier and as his chaplain and was quite prepared to distort and suppress information in order to enhance his master's achievements.

ABBÉ SUGER, a life-long friend of the French king, Louis VI (reigned 1108–37), was an important figure at the French court and had many contacts with leading men of his time. He wrote an account of Louis VI's life, probably between 1137 and 1148. Suger lived between c. 1081 and 1151.

The *Vita Ædwardi Regis* was written in 1066 by a foreign monk in honour of Queen Edith, the Confessor's wife and Earl Harold's sister, and it is written to show the excellent qualities of the Godwin family.

ORDERICUS VITALIS was born in England in 1075. His father was French but it is thought that his mother was English. When he was about ten, Orderic was sent to Normandy to become a monk. However, he always maintained a liking for England and while he had to justify the Norman Conquest he also felt compassion for the sufferings of the English under Norman rule. He wrote his long *Historia Ecclesiastica* between c. 1114 and 1141. The section on the death of William Rufus was probably written in 1135. He was very hostile to men who treated the church badly. Like William of Malmesbury, Orderic wanted to amuse his reader.

WACE was a twelfth-century romance historian who wrote to amuse and entertain. His *Roman de Rou*, commissioned by Henry II, was written between 1160 and 1170 and is largely based upon well-known works. Whilst Wace's supplements to existing histories are small and generally regarded as unreliable, he was for many years a cleric at Caen and therefore had access to local traditions.

The monk, FLORENCE OF WORCESTER, should perhaps be renamed John, for it was he who most probably wrote the chronicle using material collected together by his colleague, Florence. John wrote his history between 1124 and 1140 and had access to a version of the Anglo-Saxon Chronicle which has since been lost; as this version differed in many respects from the surviving texts, the 'Florence of Worcester' annals are of considerable historical value. The chronicle was continued until 1151.